The Observer's Pocket Series

FRESHWATER FISHES

The Observer Books

A POCKET REFERENCE SERIES
COVERING A WIDE RANGE OF SUBJECTS

Natural History
BIRDS
BIRDS' EGGS
BUTTERFLIES
LARGER MOTHS
COMMON INSECTS
WILD ANIMALS
ZOO ANIMALS
WILD FLOWERS
GARDEN FLOWERS
FLOWERING TREES
  AND SHRUBS
HOUSE PLANTS
CACTI
TREES
GRASSES
COMMON FUNGI
LICHENS
POND LIFE
FRESHWATER FISHES
SEA FISHES
SEA AND SEASHORE
GEOLOGY
ASTRONOMY
WEATHER
CATS
DOGS
HORSES AND PONIES

Transport
AIRCRAFT
AUTOMOBILES
COMMERCIAL VEHICLES
SHIPS

MANNED SPACEFLIGHT
UNMANNED
  SPACEFLIGHT
BRITISH STEAM
  LOCOMOTIVES

The Arts, etc.
ARCHITECTURE
CATHEDRALS
CHURCHES
HERALDRY
FLAGS
PAINTING
MODERN ART
SCULPTURE
FURNITURE
MUSIC
POSTAGE STAMPS
POTTERY AND
  PORCELAIN
BRITISH AWARDS
  & MEDALS
ANCIENT & ROMAN
  BRITAIN
EUROPEAN COSTUME
SEWING

Sport
ASSOCIATION FOOTBALL
CRICKET
GOLF
MOTOR SPORT

Cities
LONDON

The Observer's Book of

FRESHWATER FISHES

T. B. BAGENAL, M.A.

DESCRIBING 50 SPECIES
WITH 32 COLOUR PLATES

FREDERICK WARNE & CO. LTD.
FREDERICK WARNE & CO. INC.
LONDON • NEW YORK

ISBN 0 7232 0089 0

LIBRARY OF CONGRESS CATALOG CARD NO 76-114794

*Printed in Great Britain by
William Clowes & Sons, Limited
London, Beccles and Colchester*
229.675

Preface

Since Mr Laurence Wells wrote the first edition of this little book in 1941 there have been many changes in the study of British natural history, and perhaps the most important affecting this Observer's Book stem from research and education.

Research by professional biologists at universities as well as at Government and other laboratories is yielding more and more information about the natural history and physiology of our fishes. There is, therefore, a very great deal more known than when the Observer's Book was first written. In order to include some of this new material, much of the original text had to go, and I decided it should be completely rewritten. This is now a new book for which I must be entirely responsible.

Education in its widest sense through radio, the press and television has made more and more people aware of natural history. This up-surge of interest in wildlife of all kinds, together with a more mobile society, brings millions more people into contact with our freshwater fish. Coupled with this, education in a narrower sense has made more people able to appreciate the research of professional biologists, particularly if this is stripped of its jargon and presented in a readable form. This is what I have tried to do. In a book of this length much detail has to be lost in order to give a clear over-all account. I hope this has not also led to the loss of accuracy.

Acknowledgement is due to the National Anglers' Council and the British Record (rod-caught) Fish Committee for permission to quote the most recent record weights. Acknowledgement is also due to the following for the illustrations in this book: Grote, Vogt and Hofer's work on *The Freshwater Fishes of Central Europe* for Plates 1–10, 12–22, 25, 26, 29 and 31; Professor F. A. Smitt's work, *A History of Scandinavian Fishes*, for Plate 30; *Fishes of Great Britain and Ireland* by Francis Day, F.L.S., for Plates 27 and 32; and Mr Baz East for Plates 23, 24 and 28.

T. B. Bagenal

Contents

Introduction

This book has been written primarily with the interests of the general naturalist in mind, but it should also help the angler identify his catch. I hope it will also be of assistance in schools during natural history field work.

The arrangement for each species throughout the book has usually been the same. With some families of fish, for example with the lampreys and salmon family, there is an introductory account of the general features of the family as a whole, in which the breeding, migration or other aspects of the group are described and discussed, and in some cases put into perspective by comparison with other species only found abroad. I have tried to arrange the treatment of each species in a standard way. After a sentence or two on the status of the fish—whether it is a native or introduced; migratory or a permanent resident in freshwater—a description of the species with the weights and lengths of adults is given. Because Britain is adopting metric units, the measurements are given in centimetres and grammes with the equivalents in inches and pounds in brackets. For some fish the British rod-caught record weight is also given. These records are organised by the British Record (rod-caught) Fish Committee in cooperation with the National Anglers' Council, and they are published in avoirdupois weights. I have given the metric equivalents in brackets. In December 1968 the Committee reconsidered all past records and decided that a number would have to be discarded and that only those claims that comply with the existing rules would be allowed. Therefore there are some species which are open for claims, and the Committee has issued minimum qualifying weights, and these are given where appropriate. These records refer to fish caught by fair angling; larger fish may have been taken by other methods or found dead. These are also given if known, as are records from other countries if these are of interest.

In the description of the fish, those features that distinguish similar species have been stressed, for example the differences between gudgeon and small barbel, dace and small chub. The features given for each fish are those that will be most useful to the general naturalist and the more specialised characters that are used by the expert, such as scale counts, teeth on the pharyngeal bones and other internal features, have not been given. It is not sufficiently well known how difficult some British fish are to identify, and in some cases I have indicated that the help of an expert should be sought. The staff at the British Museum (Natural History), South Kensington, London, or at the Freshwater Biological Association's Laboratory, The Ferry House, Ambleside, Westmorland, are always willing to help with the more difficult species **provided** they are properly preserved. Neither the Post Office nor the recipients like a wet mass of stinking and rotting fish and paper. Only if the fish has been left for two or three days in methylated spirit or dilute formalin (both of which may be obtained from a chemist's shop), and only if it is then packed damp, not in liquid, in a polythene bag, should a fish be sent by post. These few and simple instructions must be obeyed; this is absolutely essential, and is all that is asked in return for the service of identifying and commenting on your fish.

After the description with lengths and weights is a statement of the habitat in which the fish is usually found. Mostly these statements are in vague terms, such as 'found in stagnant or slowly flowing waters'. This vagueness is because we do not yet know in any detail what all the factors are that influence each species in its choice of habitat. The apparent catholic tastes of the fish in their habitat preferences are probably as much due to our ignorance as to their tolerance. The water temperature, spawning sites, amount of oxygen, degree of competition with other species, water flow and food supply probably all combine together (and with other factors, some of which are within the fish itself) to define the habitats in which each species can thrive. A broad classification of habitats in which fish live has been suggested by a Belgian biologist, M. Huet.

He divided rivers into four zones depending mainly on the gradient, the current and the river width. Rivers start as very rapid streams flowing down an extremely steep gradient, and this forms the Trout Zone inhabited by trout and salmon parr and often bullheads as well. These streams join together and become small rivers, but are still steep with a rapid current, and here we have the Grayling Zone with trout, grayling, some barbel, chub, dace, gudgeon and bleak as the fish inhabitants. As the rivers descend to lower country the gradient becomes gentle and the current moderate and this is the Barbel Zone. Here the species are barbel, chub, dace, gudgeon, bleak, roach, rudd, perch, pike and eels. Finally the river becomes one with a very gentle gradient dropping with a slow current to the sea, and this is the Bream Zone with rudd, roach, perch, pike, eels, tench, bream, white bream and carp.

The trout and salmon parr of the very rapid streams and becks are able to swim fast, they cannot tolerate warm water and they require a high oxygen concentration. Fish breathe by extracting the oxygen needed for life from the water through their gills and this is analogous to the way we extract oxygen from the air through our lungs. Tench, bream and carp are able to survive in very low concentrations of oxygen that would be lethal to a trout. Many of the stagnant ponds and very slowly flowing waters inhabited by tench and bream may become seriously depleted of oxygen, particularly if there is any amount of pollution. A trout could not live in this habitat. On the other hand the lethargic tench and hump-backed carp would not be able to maintain a swimming speed necessary for survival in an upland stream.

In the remarks on breeding it will be noticed that it is often stated that the eggs of the fish from the Bream Zone are attached to aquatic weeds, and this too may perhaps be associated with oxygen requirements. During the process called photosynthesis, all green plants give out oxygen and no doubt this meets some of the oxygen needs of the embryos developing inside the fish eggs. Also the tiny fry of pike, bream and carp have little adhesive organs with which they attach themselves to the leaves of plants. It is the interplay of factors such as these that still need to be studied in much more detail before we can fully understand the habitat preferences of our freshwater fish.

Turning next to the remarks on food, some of the fish eat large amounts of vegetable matter; these include the roach, dace and minnow, but there are no completely herbivorous native British fish. Most of them supplement their diet with animal matter, particularly in winter. Some of the cyprinid fish of the lowland muddy ponds and rivers probably seek out worms and insects from the bottom to a considerable depth, and in so doing swallow a large quantity of mud from which they extract much nutritious material. Other fish, such as the trout, perch and bullhead, are almost entirely carnivorous and actively chase their prey. The pike lies in wait and makes a sudden pounce on its victim. The diets of all these fishes vary considerably from one locality to another depending largely on what is available.

One dietary feature is that our fish almost all depend at some stage on plankton, whether it be the stream plankton called drift, or animals such as *Daphnia*, the water flea. The divergence in feeding habits comes when the fish are large enough and are growing so fast that they need more substantial mouthfuls, though char and whitefish continue to thrive on a diet largely composed of plankton all their lives.

Finally under each species there is some account of the distribution both in Britain and elsewhere. Unfortunately there is not sufficient room to deal with the distribution in detail. It will be noticed that many of our freshwater fish have a wide distribution over much of Europe and Asia. What is not apparent, of course, is that there are many species present in Europe which, because of the salty barrier, are not found in Britain,

'This precious stone set in the silver sea
Which serves it in the office of a wall'.

Classified Index to
Orders, Families, Genera and Species

15

Order HAPLOMI
Family ESOCIDAE
Pike   *Esox lucius* L., 74

Order OSTARIOPHYSI
Family CYPRINIDAE
Common carp   *Cyprinus carpio* L., 80
Crucian carp   *Carassius carassius* (L.), 83
Goldfish   ,,   *auratus* (L.), 85
Barbel   *Barbus barbus* (L.), 87
Gudgeon   *Gobio gobio* (L.), 89
Tench   *Tinca tinca* (L.), 91
Minnow   *Phoxinus phoxinus* (L.), 93
Orfe   *Leuciscus idus* (L.), 95
Chub   ,,   *cephalus* (L.), 97
Dace   ,,   *leuciscus* (L.), 100
Roach   *Rutilus rutilus* (L.), 102
Rudd   *Scardinius erythrophthalmus* (L.), 104
Common bream   *Abramis brama* (L.), 106
White bream   *Blicca bjoerkna* (L.), 107
Bleak   *Alburnus alburnus* (L.), 109
Bitterling   *Rhodeus sericeus* (Pallas), 111

Family COBITIDAE
Stone loach   *Noemacheilus barbatulus* (L.), 112
Spined loach   *Cobitis taenia* L., 113

Family SILURIDAE
Wels   *Silurus glanis* L., 114

Order APODES
Family ANGUILLIDAE
Common eel   *Anguilla anguilla* (L.), 116

Order ANACANTHINI
Family GADIDAE
Burbot   *Lota lota* (L.), 118

Order PERCOMORPHI
Family SERRANIDAE
Bass   *Dicentrarchus labrax* (L.), 120

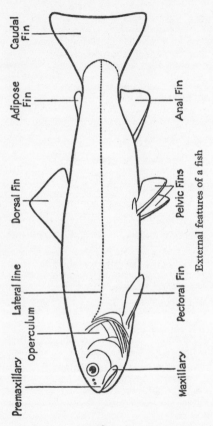

External features of a fish

Caudal Fin

Adipose Fin

Anal Fin

Dorsal Fin

Pelvic Fins

Lateral line

Pectoral Fin

Operculum

Premaxillary

Maxillary

18

The Lampreys
Family PETROMYZONIDAE

Most people will agree that the lampreys are most unattractive creatures, but they have many features that make them of very great interest to naturalists. They are not strictly fish, though they have an eel-like body; they do not have any scales, paired fins or proper jaws. Their interest to zoologists also lies in some of their other characters, for example their kidneys and nerves, which are thought to be similar to those of the ancestral vertebrates from which the fish have evolved. As well as showing some of these supposedly primitive features, the lampreys exhibit others that are very highly specialised for their particular way of life, for example their methods of feeding and nest building, which will be described later. However, although these primitive features, which give a glimpse into some of the stages through which modern fishes may have evolved, make them most attractive to zoologists, the layman usually finds them rather repugnant creatures.

The mouth, which is at the very front of the head, is surrounded by a funnel-shaped sucker which is armed with hard sharp teeth. In the mouth is a tongue, also armed with teeth, which can be brought forward to rasp away at any creature to which the lamprey may have attached itself with its sucker. In this way it is an external parasite, though sometimes it eats such a big hole in its victim that its complete head is inside.

Most fish breathe by passing water in through the mouth and out through the gills, and the function of the gills is to make an easy way for the oxygen dissolved in the water to pass into the blood of the animal. In most fish the gills are close together and covered by one flap of bone, the opercular bone, so that there is only one opening on each side through which the water passes out. Such an arrangement, in which the water is taken in through the mouth, would be difficult for the lamprey that is attached to its host by a sucker round its mouth, and which may be buried in the flesh. In lampreys there are seven separate gill openings which are supported on an elastic framework of gristle. Water is squeezed out of the gill pockets by the contraction of some muscles, and they refill by the elastic expansion of the gristle. This pumping movement, which is extremely rapid, is a very obvious feature of live lampreys.

Lampreys all have the same basic shape and can only really be confused with eels. Apart from the sucker and gill openings, which may not be immediately obvious when the animal is swimming among weeds under water, the identity of a lamprey is revealed by its lack of paired fins and the two dorsal fins on the posterior half of the fish, compared with the much larger and

continuous dorsal fin of the eel, which is joined
to the tail and anal fins.

The Sea Lamprey

Family PETROMYZONIDAE   *Petromyzon marinus*

This species is the largest British lamprey and
may grow to over 90 cm (3 ft) in length and 7·5
cm (3 in.) in thickness (Plate 1). The back and
sides have a marbled or blotchy pattern of dark
brown or olive green, while the undersides are
whitish in colour. The two dorsal fins are
distinctly separate.

The sea lamprey is the most parasitic of the
British lampreys. It spends most of its life
attached to marine fish and is said to be particularly common on basking sharks. The round
wounds, made when it is feeding, are more
commonly seen than the lamprey itself, perhaps
because it swims away when its host is
caught.

In late spring or early summer the lampreys
migrate, mainly at night, into the rivers and seek
out a place where the water is about 15 to 60 cm
(6 in. to 2 ft) deep, and where the current is swift
and the bottom is of stony sand. Here the
lampreys construct a nest, by picking up in their
suckers stones from an oval area and depositing
them round the edge so that a rim is formed.
Into this depression of a nest, the eggs are shed and
fertilised by the milt from the male. The eggs

are slightly sticky and get mixed with the sand stirred up by the spawning lampreys. The adults then move stones back on to the nest which buries the eggs still further. The adults are completely exhausted by the nest building and spawning activities, and die very shortly afterwards.

The eggs hatch out into small worm-like creatures, which although obviously of the lamprey family are blind and toothless (Plate 1). At one time it was not realised that this animal was a young lamprey and it was described as a separate species called *Ammocoetes branchialis*. These young lampreys, called ammocoete larvae, live with their heads sticking out of mud on the river bottom for a few years eating mainly the broken up remains of dead plants and animals. They then change into the adult form with eyes and teeth, and migrate down to the sea.

The sea lamprey is said to be very intolerant of pollution and is certainly very much less abundant than it used to be. In North America it became a major pest to fisheries after it gained access to the Great Lakes through the Welland Canal which by-passes the Niagara Falls. An enormous amount of research has been done to reduce this land-locked population and the numbers are now under control. Elsewhere the sea lamprey is found from Iceland, the Faeroes and Norway, southwards to the north-west coast of Africa and the Mediterranean.

The River Lamprey

Family PETROMYZONIDAE   *Lampetra fluviatilis*

The river lamprey, or lampern as it is sometimes called does not exceed 50 cm (20 in.) in length, and is rarely more than 40 cm (16 in.) long (Plate 1). In thickness it grows to about 2·5 cm (1 in.). Apart from the difference in size, it can be distinguished from the sea lamprey by its uniform brownish-green colour without any of the marbling or blotches that are characteristic of the larger species. The underside is silvery white.

In spite of the English name, most river lampreys, but possibly not all, spend much of their lives in the sea. In autumn they migrate into fresh water to spawn the following spring. After some time in fresh water, the river lamprey ceases to feed and the alimentary canal, comprising the stomach and intestines, begins to degenerate and atrophy. These lampreys tend to move further up the rivers than do the sea lampreys, and they prefer to make their nests among pebbles rather than stones. The reproductive behaviour of nest building is very similar to that of the larger species, but the nest is rather less well-defined. After spawning, the lampreys are completely emaciated and die.

Up to about 40,000 eggs are laid by one female. The larva after hatching is an ammocoete similar to that of the sea lamprey, but with less pigmentation. After about three to five years, when they have reached between 15 and 20 cm (6 and 8 in.) in length, the ammocoetes change to the adult form and migrate down river. Like the sea lamprey, they attach themselves with their suckers to fish which they eat by rasping with the teeth on their tongues.

The river lamprey is distributed in all the coastal waters of Europe from southern Greenland and Stavanger in Norway, to the Mediterranean. It is locally common throughout Britain, particularly in the fast running rivers of the west coast.

The Brook Lamprey

Family PETROMYZONIDAE   *Lampetra planeri*

This lamprey (Plate 1) has many characteristics that are very different from the two previous species. It is the smallest British lamprey and rarely exceeds 18 cm (7 in.) in length or the thickness of a pencil. The colour of the back is a uniform slate grey, brown or greenish blue and the undersides are white or silvery tinged with red. The dorsal fins are joined. The teeth are blunt and not strong.

The brook lamprey is confined entirely to fresh water and is found in the smaller rivers and clear, fast running streams. It probably spends much of its time in a burrow and only comes out to feed at night.

24

Nests, similar to those built by the two other species, are made communally, and four to eight individuals may spawn together in the same place. There is hardly any recognisable migration to the spawning area and the same place tends to be used year after year by succeeding generations.

The adults, which are smaller than the ammocoete larvae, breed in late May or early June very soon after metamorphosis. The sexual products are almost ripe in the ammocoete, which is in marked contrast to the river lamprey where the larvae are completely immature.

The ammocoetes feed on minute invertebrates and small fragments of plants and animals, but the adult cannot feed at all since the gut is atrophied and impassable for food.

The Sturgeon

Family ACIPENSERIDAE   *Acipenser sturio*

This is a rare British fish and is a native of the countries bordering on the Baltic, and of eastern Europe. It belongs to a group of fishes called the Chondrostei, and the remains of these fish are particularly abundant in the rocks that were laid down under the sea about 300 million years ago. The sturgeon is one of the very few survivors of this group and so is of particular interest to students of fish evolution.

The sturgeon (Plate 2) can grow to a very

25

large size. One taken in March 1909 in the North Sea measured 345 cm (11 ft 4 in.) and weighed 320 kg (706 lb). The appearance of the sturgeon is most unusual and cannot be confused with that of any other species. It has an elongated body which is armoured with five rows of large bony plates. These tend to make the body appear pentagonal in section. There are other large bony plates on the head, and smaller bony tubercles are scattered irregularly over the body between the rows already mentioned. The plates are half embedded in the skin, are bluntly pointed and have a texture of ivory. The snout is long and low with four barbels under the lower jaw. The tail is forked with the backbone and flesh running into the larger upper lobe as in the sharks and dogfish. The upper parts of the body are a grey-green or brownish grey, while the belly is a yellowish white or silvery. The paired fins are grey tinged with yellow.

Sturgeons enter fresh water to breed and although one or two British specimens are caught every year at sea, occasionally one is reported from fresh water, for example from the Trent or Severn.

Although sturgeon grow very quickly, reaching 35·5 cm (14 in.) in the first year, they live to an old age of 30 years or more. In spite of their large size and fast growth, most of their food is small invertebrates, though they also eat fish the size of anchovies.

In Russia, particularly at the mouth of the River Volga where sturgeons are abundant, very large numbers are caught. Not only is the flesh extremely good to eat, but also the sturgeon is famous as the source of caviar. This delicacy, which is a speciality of Russia, is made from the roes of the females. Another product that is made from sturgeons is isinglass. This is a fish gelatin, used for clarifying wine and beer, pickling and as a preservative, and is made from their swimbladders.

In Britain the sturgeon was a royal fish and all that were caught belonged to the Crown. This dated from an Act of Parliament in the reign of Edward I which has only recently been repealed, and which stated, 'the king shall have the wreck of the sea throughout the realm, whales and great sturgeons'.

The Shads

Family CLUPEIDAE

The shads belong to the family CLUPEIDAE of which the herring of the sea is the most important member. Other marine species are the sprat, pilchard and anchovy. Sardines are small canned pilchards, and brisling is the name given to small sprats when canned. There are two other British species, the allis shad and twaite shad, and these migrate into fresh water to breed.

Care has to be taken when identifying the members of this family, and all specimens found in fresh water should be preserved and sent to an expert for an opinion. Confusion arises not only because the shads are difficult to distinguish, but also because the young of the marine species, particularly the herring and sprat, often wander into fresh water at the stage when they are called whitebait.

The shads are very similar in shape to the herring, though somewhat deeper in the body and they grow to a larger size. The diagnostic difference between the herring *Clupea harengus* and the sprat *Sprattus sprattus* on the one hand, and the shads on the other, is that in the former the hinge of the lower jaw and the skull is not so far back as to be in line with the back of the eye, whereas in the shads it is, and in the shads there is a marked notch in the middle of the upper jaw which is absent in the herring, sprat and pilchard. The extent to which herrings can penetrate into fresh water is illustrated by specimens recorded in the summer of 1911 from Hamburg on the River Elbe, over 70 km (43 miles) above the limit of brackish water.

Scottish herring fishermen used to call the shad 'the king of the herrings' and they believed that he was the leader of the herring shoals. Both species of shad are supposed to be attracted to music, and W. J. Gordon says that the German shad fishermen used to hang bells on their shad nets not only to attract the fish, but also to keep them 'lost in admiration as the nets are drawn in'.

The Allis Shad

Family CLUPEIDAE   *Alosa alosa*

This is a rare fish, living mainly in the sea and estuaries but ascending rivers to spawn. It is the largest of the shads and regularly reaches over 60 cm (2 ft) in length, and specimens have been recorded which were 76 cm. (30 in.) long and had a weight of 3·629 kg (8 lb) (Plate 3).

The upper parts are bottle green or greenish blue, while the sides are silvery like a herring, but there is also a brownish or golden yellow iridescence particularly on the head. There is no lateral line down the side of the body, but the eye has a transparent membrane which covers the front and hind edge. The abdomen has 21 sharply keeled scales in front of the pelvic fins, and 16 behind. There is usually one large dark spot at the top of the gill cover and occasionally one or two behind it, but never a long row of 5 to 16 as in the next species.

These shads, which are normally solitary fish at sea, migrate into fresh water when ready to spawn after gathering in shoals in the estuaries. Spawning takes place in May or June at night in the open water of the rivers, and sometimes

29

in the brackish lower reaches. They are said to make a great commotion by splashing about on the surface. The eggs are not sticky and are only just heavy enough to sink; in sea water they float. The young migrate down to the sea after about a year when 7·5 to 12·5 cm (3 to 5 in.) long.

Shads eat plankton, the minute drifting animal life which abounds in the sea. It used to be said that the food collected on the gill-rakers, which acted as a sort of sieve and retained the small organisms as the water passed from the mouth to the gills. However this probably is not true, and the fish almost certainly feed in the same manner as herrings, that is they actually select the organisms they prefer from whatever species happen to be in the plankton at the time, and swallow each one individually. The gill rakers, however, do prevent the plankton from escaping with the water passing through the gills. In the allis shad there are from 80 to 130 long rakers on the first gill arch, whereas in the next species, the twaite shad, there are only about 40 to 60 and they are shorter and thicker.

The allis shad is distributed from northern Norway to the western part of the Mediterranean and into the Baltic. In the British Isles it used to breed in the Severn and the Shannon, but shads are very sensitive to pollution and they are certainly now a rare fish in fresh water, although they are regularly caught on the Scottish west coast and elsewhere.

The Twaite Shad

Family CLUPEIDAE   *Alosa fallax*

Like the allis shad, this is a predominantly marine
fish which migrates into fresh water to spawn,
though some varieties are found in land-locked
lakes.

The twaite shad (Plate 4) is smaller than the
allis shad. It is usually 30 to 40 cm (12 to 16 in.)
long and rarely exceeds 50 cm (20 in.). The
coloration of the two species is very similar, but
there are some 5 to 16 large dark spots on each
side of the body in a longitudinal row. The gill
rakers are smaller and less numerous in the
twaite shad as was explained under the previous
species.

The twaite shad does not move far up the
rivers, and most of the spawning takes place in
brackish estuarine waters. The eggs, which are
laid in April and May, are carried near the bottom
by the tide. The young grow rapidly and
become fully marine in the late autumn.

The twaite shad is found along the European
Atlantic coast from Trondheim in Norway, and
Iceland, to Portugal and into the Mediterranean
and Black Sea. In the Baltic it is found right
up into the Gulf of Finland. It is regularly
caught by fishing boats off the British coasts.

There are various lakes that contain land-
locked varieties of this shad, for example in
southern Switzerland and in northern Italy.
There is also a land-locked form of twaite shad

in Killarney Lake, Ireland. This variety never grows to more than 23 cm (9 in.) in length, has a deeper body and 43 to 53 gill rakers.

The Salmon Family

Family SALMONIDAE

The salmon family is by far the most important single group of freshwater fishes, not only from the point of view of angling, commercial value and culinary art, but also because more is probably known about this family of fishes, and more research is devoted to them, than any other group. The research includes not only that concerned with commercial fisheries, but also these fish have been studied extensively from the standpoint of pure zoology because the eggs and embryos are not difficult to grow and the adults are easy to keep in tanks and ponds.

The family is well represented in the British Isles in lakes and streams, and includes species that are predominantly marine and come to fresh water to spawn, and others which live all their lives in fresh water. Not only is there a great range in these habits throughout the family, but also the individual species are remarkably variable in their habits: in some localities they spend their whole lives in fresh water, while elsewhere they migrate to the sea. It is possible that the ancestral salmonids were a freshwater group in which some races developed the urge to go to the rich marine feeding grounds for their main growing period, but on the other hand there is slightly more evidence that the salmonids were originally marine fish in which some races evolved the habit of migrating to the safer fresh water in which to spawn and in which their young could pass the most vulnerable time of their lives. In the group Isospondyli, to which this family belongs, there are also other families composed of entirely marine species.

The salmonids are native throughout the northern hemisphere. Some species, however, have been successfully introduced into the southern hemisphere.

The appearance of all salmonids is very similar. They are well streamlined, elongated fish with clean lines. The fin rays are soft and the dorsal fin is rarely large (except in the grayling), and the pelvic fins are in line with it. The tail is usually well forked though in some species, for example the salmon and the trout, it becomes less so with age. One feature which is found in all the species is the adipose fin. This is a small fleshy lobe, has no fin rays, and is situated on the back near the tail. It is not a diagnostic feature of the salmonids, since it is present in the related families COREGONIDAE (whitefish), OSMERIDAE (smelts) and the ARGENTINIDAE. The completely unrelated American catfish *Ictalurus nebulosus* also has an adipose fin. The function of the adipose fin is not known and a few local races of some species have been found with the adipose fin missing. However in spite of these remarks, the adipose fin is a very useful guide to the salmonid and related families.

The British genera of the fish belonging to the group Salmonoidea may be distinguished as follows:

SALMONIDAE

Salmon and trouts (*Salmo*) The mouth in this genus is large. The species are distinguished from chars by the arrangement of the teeth on a bone in the centre of the roof of the mouth. This bone, called the 'vomer', has a row of backward pointing teeth all the way down the middle.

Chars (*Salvelinus*) This genus, which is very similar to the previous one, contains the alpine char and the brook char. The teeth on the vomer are in a little cluster at the front, and do not extend down the centre of the roof of the mouth. The scales of chars are smaller than those of trouts, and chars tend to have a pattern of light marks on a darker background, while with trout the background is paler and the markings are darker. At the breeding time they tend to become extremely colourful.

COREGONIDAE

Whitefish (*Coregonus*) The mouth is small, and the teeth, in those species that have any, are minute. Superficially these fish are more reminiscent of herrings than trout.

THYMALLIDAE

Graylings (*Thymallus*)   The fish in this genus are characterised by a very large dorsal fin which has 18 to 24 rays.

OSMERIDAE

Smelt (*Osmerus*)   Small, silvery coastal fish which enter fresh water to spawn.   The mouth is large, with large teeth.   The scales are also large.

The salmon that is found in Britain is the Atlantic salmon *Salmo salar*, and should not be confused with the Pacific salmon which belongs to the genus *Oncorhynchus*.   The Pacific salmon are typically found up the west coast of the United States and Canada, the coasts of Japan, and the Pacific coasts of Russia.   Five of the species are extremely important commercially, and it is the Pacific salmon we buy as canned salmon in Britain.   The Russians have tried to introduce one of the species, the pink salmon, into the rivers flowing into the White Sea, and stragglers from these experiments have strayed as far as Norway, and a few have even reached Britain.   It is at present very unlikely that they will become established in our rivers.   The Pacific salmon feeds in the sea, and some species breed on the intertidal beaches, and others in fresh water.   Some breeding sites involve a journey of thousands of miles up to the head-waters of the rivers. A characteristic of all the species of Pacific salmon, no matter in what type of site they breed, is that they die very soon after spawning.

The Atlantic Salmon

Family SALMONIDAE   *Salmo salar*

There can be little doubt that the adult salmon is one of the most exciting fish for the naturalist to see. Not only has this fish a really beautiful body form and firm clean lines, but it is most often seen when leaping spectacularly up water-falls to reach the spawning areas. Furthermore the sheer power and size of adult salmon makes one realise that one is seeing a fish that is second to none among our freshwater species. The only ugly feature perhaps, is the head of the male when it has developed a marked hook, or kype, on the lower jaw at spawning time (Plate 5).

In size adult salmon range up to 150 cm (60 in.) long and 38·5 kg (85 lb) in weight. The British rod-caught record stands at 64 lb (29 kg) for a salmon caught in the River Tay in 1922.

The back of the salmon is steel blue, indigo or blue-black, the sides are silvery with a steel blue or pinkish tint, and the belly is silvery white, also with a pinkish tinge which may even become red at spawning time, particularly in the males. The head, sides and upper parts are irregularly scattered with angular or cross-shaped spots. The fins are dark slate grey, and for the size of the fish, the dorsal fin is fairly small. The tail is forked in the young but becomes less so in the adults. The region just in front of the tail has a distinct handle-shaped appearance. The head is large.

Since the salmon is predominantly a marine fish which comes to fresh water to spawn, we will start the description of the life history at this latter stage. An apology must be made for the large number of names that are applied to the various stages in the salmon's life, but the local names that are given by netsmen in various parts of Britain will not be included since almost every fishing community seems to have a nomenclature of its own.

The adult salmon may run up the rivers at any time, and the fish in different rivers run at various times; for example one river may always have salmon that enter in the spring while another has autumn fish. Some of the fish ascending in late autumn may have only partly developed reproductive organs and be due to spawn almost a whole year hence. During this time while the adults are in fresh water they do not feed, and one of the mysteries of this extraordinary fish is why, when this is the case, they should so readily take the fisherman's lures.

When they come in from the sea, the salmon are well fed, and have extensive reserves of fat. This store of fat is used for two purposes. Firstly the reproductive products are ripening. In the female this involves building up the eggs which are rich in food reserves for the future embryo and fry. There may be up to 10,000 eggs in a salmon 90 cm (36 in.) long. As well as this drain on the adults, there is the requirement of providing energy to swim to the spawning grounds which may be in the headwaters of the river. Not only is there the distance over the ground to be covered, but all the time the river is flowing against them. The fish do indeed have to swim just to stay in the same place. As well as this there may be waterfalls and rapids to be negotiated. Watching salmon leaping a weir or waterfall is a wonderful sight and it is well worth while to make a visit to a waterfall when the salmon are running. They try and try again to mount the higher obstacles until they are successful, or fall back exhausted. To be successful the salmon needs to have a good pool below the fall, and it is said that its depth should equal three times the height to be leapt. A reliable record from the River Orrin in Rossshire is of a vertical leap of 11 ft 4 in. (approx. 3·5 m) from the water level in the pool below to the level in the pool above. This must have been an incredible spectacle to watch.

By October most of the fish have reached the spawning areas and are resting in the pools nearby. The spawning takes place in November or December. The females first move up to the spawning sites, which are areas of gravel in about

60 cm (2 ft) of water, and after a few exploratory excursions, they begin to make a nest or 'redd'. This is done by flicking the body over sideways and lifting the stones by the suction of the tail being flapped vigorously. After considerable digging, or 'cutting' as it is called, the hole may be 15 cm (6 in.) or more deep. In this hole the female is joined by the male and the eggs and milt are shed into it. The milt contains millions of the minute spermatozoa, one of which enters each egg and fertilises it. After the spawning, the female moves 30 cm (1 ft) or so upstream and by further cutting covers the eggs and fills in the depression. The covering up of one redd merges with the cutting of another and as many as eight may be made before the female has spawned all her eggs.

After spawning, the spent adults drop down stream towards the sea. Some survive the rigours and exhaustion of spawning, but many, particularly the males, are unable to withstand the drain on their reserves, and die. Certainly these fish, which are now known as kelts, are in a very emaciated condition, with lacerations and often covered with fungus, particularly when compared with the fat, well fed and sleek appearance they had when they first came in from the sea.

The kelts that do reach the sea start feeding again and the rich marine plankton allows them to regain condition and replace their fat reserves in preparation for another spawning migration.

The fungus and parasites they may have picked up in the river cannot stand the salt water, and this helps the salmon to recover condition quickly.

Meanwhile the eggs are developing under the gravel in the redds. In about 100 days (depending on the temperature of the water) the young salmon hatches and at this stage is called an alevin. Some time before hatching the young embryo will have been visible inside the egg, and the dark pigment of the eyes is particularly noticeable. When the alevin emerges from the egg it is only about 1·5 cm (½ in.) long, and still has a large amount of the egg yolk to provide it with nourishment. These little fish remain safe 20 cm (8 in.) or more down in the gravel. They have two main instincts, one is to keep away from the light, and the other is to snuggle into crevices. This keeps them deep down in the gravel for a further month until all the yolk has been used up in growth. Only then does the little fish—now called a fry—come up into the outer world and start to feed on the minute animals, particularly those drifting down in the current. By this time the scales are beginning to grow and the little salmon really does look like a fish. Growth is not particularly rapid; they may take two years or more to reach 15 cm (6 in.) in length. After about 7·5 cm (3 in.), the little fish develop 10 or 11 dark vertical bands on each side of the body. The fish is now called a parr (Plate 6), and the dark bands are called the parr-marks. The male parr often becomes sexually mature and they are regularly seen with the large adult male and female salmon in the spawning redds. The length of time the young salmon remain in fresh water varies considerably. Some migrate in their second summer, while the more slow growing ones of the northern rivers do not migrate until their fourth summer or even later. Before migrating as smolts, the young fish develop a silvery layer on their scales which in time completely covers the parr-marks. The silvery deposit is an excretionary product and it is a sign of the considerable internal physiological changes that are taking place in the fish that will enable it to pass from fresh water to marine conditions.

Once the salmon pass into the sea very little is known about them. Apart from those caught in the nets as they are congregating to move in to spawn, they are rarely caught by commercial fishermen in British waters, and until recently the habits of the salmon at sea were completely unknown. However in 1965 very large salmon feeding grounds were found off western Greenland. Since that date an enormous gill-net fishery has grown up, and indeed so many are caught that there are fears for the future of the species. These feeding grounds are in international waters, so the regulation of the fishery is difficult and requires international agreement. Some species of whales have been hunted almost to extinction because it was impossible to get all nations involved to agree on a reasonable limit to their catches. We can only hope that the nations that can regulate the Greenland salmon fishery will take adequate action together before it is too late.

The length of time that salmon spend at sea, like that in fresh water, varies considerably. Many fish return to breed after only one year, in which case they are called 'grilse', but many stay for four years or more and return as fully grown salmon.

One of the great mysteries in the life of the salmon arises from the fact that the majority of the fish—though certainly not all—return to spawn in the rivers that they themselves left as smolts. We have no idea how the salmon manages to sense which is the right river, and we have no idea how it can navigate over thousands of miles of ocean to reach that river.

The salmon is found round the Atlantic Ocean, from Massachusetts to Labrador on the American side, through Greenland and Iceland, and from the White Sea and Scandinavia to south-western France on the European side. The salmon extends into the Baltic, but not into the Mediterranean. In Britain the salmon was once much more widespread than it is now. Many suitable salmon rivers, such as the Thames, have been ruined for this species by pollution, so that now the salmon is only found in rivers that have clean, well-oxygenated water all the way down to the sea.

The salmon is attacked by a number of parasites. In fresh water they may become infested with the gill maggot *Salmincola salmonea* which is a crustacean copepod. This creature infects the salmon mainly when the river is low and the fish have congregated in a small pool waiting for sufficient water to allow them to migrate up stream. These gill maggots can remain alive on the fish even when they return to the sea. They feed on the blood of the fish as it passes through the gills.

Another parasite is the freshwater louse *Argulus foliaceus*. These animals attach themselves by two suckers and they also feed on the blood of the fish. In the sea there is yet another parasite that is said to be a blood sucker. This is the sea louse *Lepeophtheirus salmonis*. The creature does not attach itself with suckers, but can move about the skin and hold on by means of two claws that are dug into the flesh. The sea louse cannot survive in fresh water so its presence is often taken to indicate that the salmon are freshly run from the sea. However the parasite has been recorded on salmon 193 km (120 miles) from the sea and it has been suggested that in cold water the louse may remain alive for a week on the fish.

The damage that these parasites do through their consumption of blood is probably not very significant unless they are present in very large numbers, but they may do more damage by making sites for disease and fungus infection. This may be an important factor in the mortality of kelts.

The Trout

Family SALMONIDAE   *Salmo trutta*

The trout is probably the best known British
freshwater fish, and it is certainly one of the most
popular sport-fish with anglers. It is very
common and widespread and a great deal is
known about its natural history. Because it is
easy to rear and to keep in ponds, it has been
much studied by zoologists. However it is what
we might describe as a very plastic species, that
is, it is extremely variable in its habits and is
adaptable to a wide range of conditions so that
almost anything we can say about it in one
locality could be contradicted by its habits
somewhere else.

This great variability has led in the past to a
great many varieties of trout being described and
many of these have been considered by some
authorities to be different species. The biggest
difference within the trout group is that between
the sea trout, which spend most of their lives in
the sea and only come to fresh water to breed
(Plate 7), and the non-migratory brown trout
that live in fresh water all their lives (Plate 8).
The life history of the sea trout is very similar to
that of the salmon, but the non-migratory brown
trout of streams and rivers behave, and look,
completely different. However these are not
justifiable reasons for calling them different
species. It is difficult to produce an all embrac-
ing definition of a species, but the basis of modern

44

ideas of what constitutes a species is that it is a group of organisms which produce fertile offspring, and that one species differs from another when the progeny (if any) are sterile. Another basic consideration when deciding if two varieties belong to the same species is that the differences between them must not be the product of their different environments.

When we apply these criteria to trout we find that the eggs of the sea trout can be fertilised by the milt of brown trout, and the progeny of this 'cross' are themselves fertile. The 'cross' can also be made the other way with the eggs of brown trout, with similar results. Turning to the other criterion, sea trout can be reared to maturity in ponds and these fish would migrate if they were allowed to, but their offspring tend to lose this urge. Furthermore it was found that when brown trout were introduced into New Zealand and the Falkland Islands, some developed a migratory habit. On some islands round Britain true freshwater fish are completely absent, but there are many native brown trout and eels. The only reasonable explanation for the presence of these trout is that they are the descendants of trout that have come from the sea.

It seems, therefore, that we must treat sea trout and brown trout as belonging to the same species. This does not mean that they are exactly the same. Some of the progeny of a brown trout × sea trout cross turn out to be migratory and others do not, so it is probable

45

that their habits are carried genetically from one generation to the next, but that there are mutations, or spontaneous changes, between both varieties of trout. On the other hand the difference between brown trout and sea trout does not appear to be a completely all-or-nothing character. Even the small brown trout of a moorland beck tend to migrate a small way upstream to spawn, and those in a river often move into the tributary streams, and the lake trout move into the inflowing rivers. Also there are some trout which, while not real 'sea' trout, move down to the estuaries and are called 'slob trout'. In spite of these graduations between the brown and sea varieties, there is a marked difference when the young sea trout becomes silvery like a salmon smolt, and migrates to the sea, leaving the brown trout in residence behind.

The trout can grow to a length of over 100 cm (39 in.) and a weight of more than 15 kg (about 33 lb). The British rod-caught record for a brown trout is 18 lb 2 oz (8·221 kg) for one caught in Loch Garry in 1956; the record for a sea trout is open at 20 lb (9·072 kg). The size to which trout grow is very variable and is clearly dependent on where they live, and being such an adaptable and plastic fish, they have a wide range of habitats. Those that live all their lives in a mountain stream grow very slowly, and may for example be only 23 cm (9 in.) long when they are seven years old. On the other hand, the trout in a lake such as Windermere in the Lake District, have an average length of 48 cm (19 in.) at the same age. The rate of growth from different waters is given (in centimetres) below:

	Age (years)						
	1	2	3	4	5	6	7
A northern moorland beck	4·8	8·7	13·5	16·3	19·8	21·6	23·7
A southern chalk stream	10·2	25·4	33·0	40·6	48·3	—	—
A southern acid stream	6·0	12·7	17·8	21·9	28·0	28·8	—
A northern lake	5·8	13·7	21·6	28·5	35·9	40·6	48·3

The growth of trout is very dependent on temperature and the growth in the south is faster than in the colder north, but there are many other factors involved as well; for example, trout feed by sight and the days are longer during the northern summer than in the south, so there is a longer time for the fish to be foraging. The most striking point in the above figures is the very fast growth in the southern chalk stream. The reason for this fast growth in the hard waters of the chalk streams is not yet known, and there are many interacting factors that are difficult to separate. For instance, there tend to be more other fish species competing with the trout for food in the chalk streams, but on the other hand there are often grossly overcrowded populations of trout in the soft water streams. The greater production of food, and the larger variety of food species available, are certainly some of the most important factors, but they are not the only ones, and the actual chemistry of the water in relation to the chemistry of the fish may also be important.

Not only do the lake trout grow faster and larger than those in an upland beck, but also they live longer. The oldest trout caught in Windermere had reached an age of 16 years.

In the same way that the length of the trout varies in different waters, so also does their appearance. The basic pattern is that the back is dark, bluish-grey, olive, brown or blue-black, and the undersides are silvery white (Plate 8). The sides tend to have a golden or silvery sheen, and the sides and belly can have a great deal of yellow. All the upper parts of the fish are covered with blue, red or brown spots which may have a distinct grey or blue halo. The small mountain trout tend to be olive-green, well spotted and with much yellow (Plate 8), while those from peaty, or muddy streams and bog pools are dark coloured, and the Welsh black-finned trout, once called *Salmo nigripinnis* is of this variety. An Irish variety, the gillaroo, at one time named *S. stomachicus*, has a yellowish back with large brown spots and yellow underparts tinted with pink. The trout from Loch Leven in Scotland have been called *S. levenensis* and they are silvery with black spots but almost devoid of red ones. The red colour of trout depends on the presence of a pigment called carotene in their diet. Since the trout cannot make it themselves, this substance is mainly supplied in the crustacea that

48

they eat in the form of water shrimps and plankton. The Loch Leven trout are reported not to eat crustacea or molluscs.

Another variety, in this case a very large brown trout, is the one that has been called the great lake trout *S. ferox*. This variety, shows some change in shape, but these changes affect all large trout and are not characteristic of one variety. In large trout the eye does not grow quite in proportion to the rest of the body and it looks smaller; the tail, as with a growing salmon, becomes more square-ended as the notch becomes less marked, and the males develop longer heads and sharper snouts with a kype (hooked lower jaw).

The most marked colour variations, however, are in the sea trout (Plate 7) and the sewen, which is a Welsh variety. In these the back and sides are silvery with cross- or star-shaped black spots. There are often few, if any, red or blue spots on the sea trout, particularly in the female. The male is more colourful and develops a pink belly at spawning time. Large adult sea trout may very easily be confused with salmon. The form of the trout is stockier and less graceful than the salmon, its tail is less forked. The most certain way of distinguishing trout from salmon is to count the number of scales from the back of the adipose fin obliquely downwards and forwards to the lateral line. In the salmon there are 10 to 13 scales and in the trout there are 13 to 16. There are also differences in the teeth on the vomer bone in the roof of the mouth, but if identification requires examination of this it is time for the general naturalist to call in an expert.

The breeding of trout is in many ways similar to that which we have described for the salmon. In September and early October the trout begin to move up towards the spawning grounds; the sea trout run up from the sea, and the lake trout move into the feeder streams, and these movements usually coincide with a spate or freshet. The females make their nests—or redds—in much the same way as salmon do, but the spawning beds are composed of smaller gravel. The females cut the redds to between 7·5 and 10 cm (3 or 4 in.) deep and when this depression has been made the female is joined by the male. The eggs and sperm are extruded at the same time, and the eggs are fertilised. The females then cover the eggs by moving gravel in from upstream, and this may be the beginning of cutting another redd. The number of eggs laid by a female trout varies from well under a hundred in a small moorland trout to several thousand in a large lake trout. After spawning, the fish drop downstream or return to the lake or the sea. One feature of the sea trout when in fresh water is that, unlike the salmon, it feeds, and perhaps as a result of this there is not the great mortality after spawning that there is with salmon.

Trout eggs may be artificially fertilised so that the eggs and young may be incubated in a hatchery. First the eggs are squeezed from the female by a firm but gentle pressure directed backwards along the belly from the pectoral fins to the vent. This process is termed 'stripping'. The eggs are then fertilised with milt expressed from the male in a similar manner. At first the fertilised eggs are slightly sticky, but in a few minutes they come free with a gentle rocking of the dish, and may be kept in trays in running water.

The rate of development of trout eggs depends on the temperature of the water they are in, and of course in the stream bed this varies from year to year and through the winter. In general, however, eggs laid in mid-November will become 'eyed' (that is the dark pigment of the eyes of the embryo will be visible inside the egg) by about the New Year, and will hatch in late February or early March. The young trout— called alevins—hide in the dark amongst the gravel. Like salmon alevins, they have a large yolk sac which contains their nourishment for another month or six weeks, after which they will come up to the gravel surface and start to feed. Young trout fry, as they are now called, are more territorial than salmon at this stage. Each trout fry likes to have an area about 20 cm (8 in.) by 20 cm (8 in.) as a feeding territory. At this time they are about 2·5 cm (1 in.) long. The orange-red colour of the egg yolk passes into the fry and contributes to the red spots and red adipose fin that are characteristic of trout. As the fry grow they develop parr marks like salmon.

The trout parr may be distinguished from salmon by the red pigment in the adipose fin, a less forked tail, a thicker and more stocky region in front of the tail making it appear less of a 'handle', smaller pectoral fins and the jaw bone (the maxilla) extending to beyond a line vertically below the back of the eye, whereas in salmon it extends until roughly in line with the pupil. These differences are each very slight in themselves but add up to make fish clearly distinguishable—particularly if both are present for comparison at the same time, and there are a number of specimens to examine.

Some trout parr develop into a stage similar to the salmon smolt by becoming more silvery and the two species are then not at all easy to distinguish, other than by the length of the maxilla relative to the eye or by a scale count. Sea trout smolts do not go so far out to sea as salmon and some run up in the autumn after only a few months in marine conditions. The adult sea trout remain near the coast and often keep in estuaries or near the mouths of rivers or burns. Those parr that remain as brown trout in fresh water slowly lose their parr marks as they take on their adult colouring.

The food of trout has been extensively studied. Trout are carnivores, but the kind of animals they eat changes as they grow older. As fry they feed mainly on larval aquatic insects, particularly midge larvae, mayfly nymphs and caddis larvae, but they also eat the larvae of other flies and of beetles, and water shrimps. Most of this food is picked up as it drifts downstream towards the fry. As the fish grow, the midge larvae become less important and in their second year, as parr, terrestrial animals such as earthworms and beetles become more important. Slowly their dependence on the drifting animals may be lessened, particularly when they take to feeding on bottom creatures such as the pea mussel. Although they may be very selective, trout have to eat what is available at the time, and because different insects, such as the mayfly, hatch at certain times, the fish, as all trout fishermen know, rise to these particular insects almost to the exclusion of everything else. In lakes and ponds the trout eat snails, water skaters and freshwater shrimps, as well as larvae of midge and caddis, and stonefly nymphs. As they grow larger they also eat fish such as minnow, perch, sticklebacks, gudgeon, loach, bullhead, eel and young salmon and trout. With large lake trout, fish is the most important part of their diet. In rivers the trout are very partial to terrestrial animals such as earthworms, caterpillars and slugs particularly when the river is in flood.

The trout is indigenous to Europe, North Africa and north-western Asia. Sea trout are found round Iceland, Scandinavia to the White Sea and into the Baltic, round the British Isles, in the North Sea, English Channel, and as far south as northern Spain. Brown trout live in the lakes and river systems that flow into these seas, and also in some of the rivers draining into the Mediterranean, but sea trout are not found there. Trout are present as separate subspecies in the Black Sea, the Caspian and Aral Sea, and extend as far south-east in the rivers as Afghanistan. The Caspian Sea trout have been known to reach a weight of 51 kg (1 cwt).

Trout have been carried from their natural range to many parts of the world. We have already mentioned their introduction into New Zealand and the Falkland Islands. They are now present in Australia (in Victoria and New South Wales), Tasmania, South Africa, Kenya, Tanzania, Argentina, Chile, Newfoundland, eastern Canada and Vancouver Island, and the United States.

The Rainbow Trout

Family SALMONIDAE   *Salmo gairdneri*

The rainbow trout (Plate 9) is a native of the river systems from southern California to south-eastern Alaska. In some ways the situation is similar to that of the European brown trout because in the United States there are numerous varieties of this species, some of which migrate to the sea and others which do not. The steelhead and cut-throat trout varieties migrate and the rainbows do not, though they are all the same species. Various races have been imported into Britain from about 1880 onwards and have become intermingled with each other, so that here we need only consider the one entity. In Britain the rainbow trout grows to 25 to 50 cm (10 to 20 in.) long. The British rod-caught record stands at 10 lb 4 drms (4·543 kg) for one caught at King's Lynn in 1970.

The back is a dark green, blue-green or grey-green. The sides are paler with a broad pink or purple iridescent band running along each side from the head to the tail. The undersides are lighter, usually silvery. The head, back, sides, dorsal, adipose and tail fins are covered with small dark spots. The pectoral and pelvic fins are often light brown, grey or pinkish. The body shape is similar to that of the brown trout, and the maxilla bone extends beyond the eye.

The rainbow trout is at once distinguishable from the brown trout by the numerous brown spots referred to above. These spots are often still clearly visible on cooked specimens that have come from the deep freeze cabinet.

This species is imported into Britain because it is a very much faster growing fish than our native brown trout, so it is ideal for trout farms. Since it grows to a marketable size in two years, the financial return on pond space is greater. It is also imported for stocking waters to be fished, because it is a good sport fish. However many of the rainbow trout that have been stocked have developed migratory habits, so that after the owner has gone to all the trouble of importing and hatching the eggs, rearing the young, and growing

55

them to a moderate size, the rainbows have suddenly disappeared to the sea.

The breeding season is in the spring, mainly from January to late March, which is useful to hatchery keepers since it comes after the brown trout, when the equipment is no longer needed for them. Although it is a hardy species, it very rarely breeds successfully in the wild in Britain, other than in a very few localities. For this reason, constant restocking is necessary to maintain the numbers. The males are said to assist in cutting the redds. The eggs are smaller than those of brown trout, and the fish often mature in their second year, and more generally in their third.

The food of rainbow trout is the same as that of brown trout, mostly insects and other invertebrates, but the larger specimens also eat fish.

The distribution is very patchy and depends mainly on where this species has been recently introduced.

The Brook Char

Family SALMONIDAE   *Salvelinus fontinalis*

This fish is often wrongly called the brook trout, but it is not a trout—it is a char (Plate 9). Not only does it have the anatomical character of char in its arrangement of the teeth on the vomer bone in the roof of the mouth (see page 59), but a glance at Plate 9 shows two other typical char characters: the very distinct white leading edge to the pectoral, pelvic and anal fins, and the pattern of light spots on a darker background rather than dark spots on a lighter background.

The brook char is a native of eastern North America and has been imported into Britain regularly since about 1889. In most cases it does not establish itself as a breeding community, but in a few places it has managed to thrive and continues to maintain itself without restocking.

The brook char is a very beautiful fish. The back is dark olive green with a paler marbled pattern. The dorsal fin is pale with brown stripes and marbling. The tail fin has several vertical brown bands. The white leading edges on the pectoral, pelvic and anal fins are followed by a black stripe (this black stripe is not present on the common char *Salvelinus alpinus*). The belly is sometimes whiteish, but more often yellowish pink or red. The sides are covered with some red spots and numerous pale ones.

In Britain this species grows to about 41 cm (16 in.), but fish of 20 to 30 cm (8 to 12 in.) in length are more common.

In America some of the brook char remain in fresh water and others migrate to the sea. Some of those that have been introduced to Britain are said to have disappeared remarkably quickly; possibly they could have escaped to the river and descended to the sea.

In Britain the brook char breed at the same time as brown trout, in late October or early

57

November. Redds are made in the gravelly bottom of swift flowing streams and the eggs, after being fertilised, are covered with more gravel. The eggs, at 4 mm in diameter, are smaller than those of brown trout.

In Britain there are isolated localities in the Lake District, Scotland and elsewhere that support thriving populations, but this fish is not easily acclimatised to our conditions.

In the United States and Canada the brook char is distributed in the Hudson Bay watershed, Quebec, Newfoundland, Nova Scotia, New Brunswick and northern New England, and is one of the most important sport fishes. An enormous amount of research has been carried out on this species by American fishery scientists.

The Char

Family SALMONIDAE   *Salvelinus alpinus*

The British chars (Plate 10) are all considered to be varieties of the arctic char, which is a species with a very wide distribution in the northern hemisphere. It is thought that at the time of the last Ice Age it had a very much wider southern distribution, with char that spent much of their time feeding in the sea and which ran up the rivers to spawn. After the retreat of the ice, the sea-run char became more and more confined to the north, but isolated populations were left in certain lakes. In some of these the char have become extinct, but in others thriving populations remain. The char is a fish that likes colder water conditions than most other salmonids, so it is restricted to those lakes in mountainous country with deep, yet well-oxygenated, water. Because the populations have been isolated from each other for many thousands of years, they have tended to develop along separate lines, and they show slight variations from one lake to another.

The char grow to a size of 40 cm (16 in.), but the size and shape of the fish is sometimes characteristic of the particular lake population. The British rod-caught record stands at 1 lb 11 oz (765 g). Char are typical salmonid fish with an adipose fin, but they are distinguishable from trout by the white leading edge to the pectoral, pelvic and anal fins, and this character is often noticeable even when one only has a glimpse of the fish swimming in the distance. The lighter spots on a darker background, and the small scales, are also usually very easily seen. The most important difference between trout and char is, however, that the former has a row of teeth on the vomer bone down the centre of the roof of the mouth, whereas in char they are in a small cluster towards the front. The char is distinguishable from the brook char (*S. fontinalis*) by its more distinctly forked tail, lack of marbling on the back, and the red spots which are plain, whereas in the brook char they have a blue halo.

The colour of the upper parts tends to be a dull blue-black, indigo, brown, or olive-green, grading to silvery orange, or pinkish white underparts in the female. In the male the underparts are extremely colourful, particularly at the spawning season, and may be pink, orange, light vermilion, crimson, or even a deep brick red. The pectoral, pelvic and anal fins are pinkish red with a very noticeable white leading edge, and the dorsal fin is grey without any of the marbling of the brook char. The spots on the upper parts are red and light pink or buff, but never black. The colours of the char are, however, very variable depending not only on the maturity of the fish and the nearness of the spawning season, but also on the particular lake population to which the fish belongs.

The char is distributed throughout northern North America, Greenland, Iceland, Spitzbergen, northern Norway and northern Siberia as varieties which feed in the sea and run up rivers to spawn, and the distribution extends further south as completely freshwater varieties into New Brunswick, northern New England, Britain, the Alps and the U.S.S.R. In Britain, therefore, the chars are restricted to their particular lakes or the rivers flowing in, and they never go to the sea. As we have already said, they are particularly associated with deep cold, well-oxygenated waters, but also some varieties ascend from the lakes to spawn in the inflowing rivers.

The differences between the various varieties of char are small and are mostly variations in shape which are difficult to define. Other differences are found in the number and size of the gill rakers. These gill rakers are the forward projecting spines on the bones that carry the gills and protect these delicate organs from damage. Gill rakers are usually well developed in fish, such as the char and herring, that live on small planktonic food particles.

In England char are only found in the Lake District, where they inhabit Windermere, Buttermere, Coniston Water, Crummock Water, Derwentwater, Ennerdale Water, Goat's Water and Haweswater. In Wales char are found in a lake in Montgomeryshire and Llyn Padarn and Llyn Peris near Llanberis. In Scotland they are found in Kirkcudbrightshire, and in numerous lochs throughout the highlands, particularly in Ross and Cromarty and in Sutherland. There is one population of char on the Isle of Lewis in the Outer Hebrides.

In Ireland the char has been reported from 36 loughs, mainly in counties Clare, Donegal and Galway, though they are also found in counties Kerry, Longford, Mayo and Wicklow. However many of the records are based on a few specimens caught many years ago, and the present distribution is not clear, particularly as several of the Irish populations are known to have died out. It is also known that there were populations at one time in Loch Hellyal in Hoy in the Orkney Islands, and another in Ullswater in the Lake District, but they are now extinct.

The spawning of char takes place from

November to March and the different populations have different times and spawning habits. Some spawn in the gravel beds in the lakes they inhabit, either in the shallow water or deeper parts, and others run up the inflowing rivers and make redds in much the same way as salmon do (for details, see that species). The eggs are smaller than those of trout and a 28 cm (11 in.) char will lay about 950.

In Russia the char that migrate from the sea have forms, like the salmon, that run in the autumn and others that run in the spring. It is interesting that in at least one British lake, Windermere, some of the wholly freshwater char spawn in the autumn and others spawn in the spring. However, we know very little about the evolution of breeding habits in char, and it would not be justifiable to jump to the conclusion that the autumn and spring spawning stocks are derived from sea-running fish which migrated at these times.

The food of the char is variable; for the most part they eat plankton (that is, the minute animal life that drifts in the main body of the lake water, such as some insects and crustacea), but also they have been recorded as consuming bottom living molluscs and crustacea.

In the introduction to the family *Salmonidae*, we said that the coloration, behaviour, spawning habits and indeed the whole biology of all the species, were incredibly variable. This variability has been well illustrated by what has been said so far about char. One thing which does not seem to vary, and which appears to apply to all the forms, is that char hold an extraordinary fascination for all who come across them—and this is not based only on their delicate flavour which makes them held in high regard when potted for breakfast. Char fishing is a highly specialised art and its practitioners become addicts. Perhaps their fascination depends to a large extent on the beauty of the fish.

The Whitefish

Family COREGONIDAE

This family is made up of three groups, the lavaret, the vendace, and the houting. The classification of the first two groups and their relationship with similar fish in Europe and in America are very complex indeed and almost all of the best qualified specialists have come up with a different classification and alternative scientific names for the fish.

However, the situation is not as difficult or as bleak as the above facts may suggest, because each of the separate varieties is found in its own circumscribed body of water. Thus if you know that the specimen has come from Derwentwater in the Lake District, you know it is the Cumberland vendace, and if your fish was obtained from the bonny banks of Loch Lomond, you know it is a lavaret called the powan.

The coregonids superficially resemble the herring in general appearance—and they have sometimes been called the 'freshwater herring'—but the presence of the adipose fin at once distinguishes them for what they are. They are recognisable from true salmonids by their larger scales, larger dorsal fin and very deeply forked tail fin, and smaller mouth with minute teeth (some varieties have no teeth at all). Confusion is really more likely between the coregonids and coarse fish such as the dace. Indeed, in one locality the schelly is confused with the chub. However, the adipose fin at once distinguishes the coregonid from any other coarse fish with which it might be confused.

In Britain the whitefish are of very little interest other than to naturalists living near the shores of the few lakes they inhabit, so the treatment here will be very brief. By contrast, in North America, and also in Switzerland and in Russia, they are of considerable commercial importance, to the extent that there are large hatcheries in which they are artificially bred and liberated in great numbers to maintain the fishery.

In Britain whitefish mostly live in lakes in isolated populations, while in Russia and elsewhere in northern latitudes, there are species which are marine and run into fresh water to breed like salmon. The situation is therefore rather like that of the char, and whitefish may be

Pl. 1

1. Brook Lamprey (p. 24)
3. Sea Lamprey (p. 21)

2. Ammocoete larva (p. 22)
4. River Lamprey (p. 23)

Sturgeon (p. 25)

Pl. 2

Allis Shad (p. 29)

Pl. 3

Twaite Shad (p. 31)
Houting (p. 68)

Pl. 4

Pl. 5

Atlantic Salmon, male and female (p. 36)

Salmon parr (p. 40)
Smelt (p. 72)

Pl. 6

Sea Trout, male and female (p. 44)

Pl. 7

Brown Trout, showing colour variations

Pl. 8

Rainbow Trout (p. 54)
Brook Char (p. 56)

Pl. 9

Char, showing colour variation (p. 58)

Pl. 10

Lavaret (Powan)
Vendace (Pollan)

Pl. 11

Pl. 12   Grayling (dwarf)   Grayling (normal) (p. 69)   Grayling (yearling)

Pike (p. 74)
Young Pike

Pl. 13

Common Carp (p. 80)

Pl. 14

Crucian Carp (p. 83)

Pl. 15

Pl. 16

Barbel, showing colour variation (p. 87)

Gudgeon (p. 89)
Stone Loach (p. 112)
Spined Loach (p. 113)

Pl. 17

Tench (p. 91)

Pl. 18

Pl. 19

Dace (p. 100)   Chub (p. 97)   Minnow (p. 93)

Roach (p. 102)
Rudd (p. 104)

Pl. 20

Common Bream (p. 106)

Pl. 21

White or Silver Bream (p. 107)
Bleak (p. 109)

Pl. 22

Bitterling, female and male (p. 111)

Pl. 23

Wels or Catfish (p. 114)

Pl. 24

Common Eel (p. 116)

Pl. 25

Pl. 26   Burbot, showing dark and light varieties (p. 118)

Bass (p. 120)

Pl. 27

Zander or Pike-perch (p. 121)
Large-mouthed Black Bass (p. 127)

Pl. 28

Perch (p. 123)
Ruffe or Pope (p. 125)

Pl. 29

Pl. 30

Thick-lipped Grey Mullet (p. 128)

Bullhead or Miller's Thumb (p. 130)

Sticklebacks:
Three-spined (p. 132) Ten-spined (p. 134)

Pl. 31

Flounder (p. 135)

Pl. 32

residual populations, derived from one or more ancestral sea-running species at the time of the last Ice Age, which became, in effect, land-locked when the climate ameliorated. Now they are found in very restricted locations and each population has tended to develop in its own way. It may perhaps be significant that many of the lakes which contain whitefish also support (or used to support) populations of char.

The Lavaret

Family COREGONIDAE   *Coregonus lavaretus*

This group for which the name 'lavaret' has been suggested, consists in Britain of three populations of similar fish which are best regarded as belonging to the same species. The main difference between them is that they are found in different lakes. They are the powan, the schelly and the gwyniad.

THE POWAN (Plate 11)

The back is slate blue-grey or grey-green, and the sides are silvery with a touch of yellow. The belly is white or silvery. The scales are large. The powan ranges up to 41 cm (16 in.) in length and lives to about ten years of age. The British rod-caught record stands at 1 lb 7 oz (652 g).

The powan is found in Loch Lomond and Loch Eck. The fish spawn in late December or January on a shallow gravel bottom. The eggs hatch about two months after being fertilised. The powans are mainly plankton feeders, that is,

65

they eat the drifting crustacea and insects in the main body of the loch, but also they eat some molluscs, insects and crustacea from the bottom (up to 14% of their food). They only take a few insects from the surface, so it is rare for them to be caught by trout anglers.

THE SCHELLY

This fish is very similar indeed to the powan in its general habits and appearance, but it has a few black spots on the upper parts that are not present on the powan. The schelly is found in Ullswater, Haweswater and Red Tarn in the Lake District, all of which flow eventually into the River Eden. It grows to 41 cm (16 in.) in length and lives to about nine years of age. The British rod-caught record is at 1 lb 7½ oz (866 g). It spawns in mid-January on a sandy bottom. Like the powan, schelly are mainly plankton feeders, but they also feed on insects in weed beds and on their own eggs at spawning time. Their flesh is delicious, especially when smoked. Fresh schelly have a most characteristic and strong smell of cucumbers.

THE GWYNIAD

This variety is the Welsh equivalent of the powan and schelly, and is found in Llyn Tegid (Lake Bala). It is smaller than the other two and has a relatively larger eye. The British rod-caught record stands at 1 lb 4 oz (567 g). It forms large shoals in mid water of the lake. The small ones are said to eat bottom living animals, and the larger gwyniad feed on plankton.

The Vendace

Family CoREGONIDAE   *Coregonus albula*

The vendace fall into two groups: the vendace of Cumberland and Lochmaben, which differ only slightly; and the pollans of Ireland which are only a little more distinct.

The Cumberland vendace are found in Derwentwater and Bassenthwaite Lake; and in southern Scotland others are found in Castle Loch and Mill Loch near Lochmaben. These are slimmer fish than the lavarets and the snout is more elongated and pointed. The back is greenish blue or blue-black, the flanks are silver with a yellowish tint and the belly is white.

Vendace grow to 20 to 23 cm (8 to 9 in.) in length. There is a story, which is now quite discredited, that the Lochmaben vendace were brought over by Mary Queen of Scots from France in 1565. Not only are vendace very delicate fish and extremely unlikely to survive such a journey in those days, but also this variety is not found on the Continent.

Vendace spawn earlier than the other whitefish, from mid-December to early January. The fish are predominantly plankton feeders. It is quite remarkable how these fish can exist in a lake which is regularly fished by trout fishermen, and has many boats crossing its surface, and yet their presence in large numbers remains almost unknown, so much so that some people say they are extinct.

THE POLLAN (Plate 11)

The pollans, which are found in Lough Neagh, Lough Erne and some lakes on the Shannon, are distinguishable from the vendace by their jaws which are of equal length, whereas the lower jaw in the other vendace group projects slightly beyond the upper. Their coloration is very similar to the vendace and they often grow to 23 to 29 cm (9 to 11 in).

The Houting

Family COREGONIDAE   *Coregonus oxyrinchus*

This is a very rare species that lives in the sea and runs up into fresh water to spawn on sand and gravel bottoms. It is at once distinguishable by its long and pointed snout which extends some way beyond the mouth (Plate 4). The upper parts are blue-grey or olive-green, and the sides are silvery with a pearly iridescence. During the breeding season, which is in November and December, the males develop white tubercles along the sides of the body.

The houting is a Continental coastal fish of the North Sea and western Baltic. In Britain it can only be classed as a vagrant, being occasionally reported from south-east England in estuaries or tidal waters.

The average size is 30 to 35 cm (12 to 14 in.), but they do grow to over 50 cm (20 in.).

The Grayling

Family THYMALLIDAE   *Thymallus thymallus*

The grayling (Plate 12) is a fish that bridges the
gap between 'game fish' and 'coarse fish'. Unlike the whitefish, grayling are fairly well known
as they have a widely scattered distribution
through England and Scotland, and because
of this they are fairly regularly caught by anglers.

The grayling looks at first sight like a darker
and more metallic version of a whitefish, with a
large dorsal fin. The adipose fin at once
associates it with the salmonid and coregonid
families, but the large scales are more reminiscent
of the latter.

The body is long and the mouth is below a
pointed and projecting snout. The back and
upper parts are grey-green, blue-grey or purple,
and the sides and belly are silvery with a metallic
brassy, or iridescent green sheen. There are
black spots scattered over the back and sides,
particularly towards the head. However, the
most conspicuous feature is the high and long
dorsal fin which has horizontal rows of dark
spots and, at the hind edge, a large blue-purple
patch. The pectoral fin is pinkish or yellow, and
the anal fin is purple. Zig-zag lines of dark
pigment accentuate the lines of the scales. The
young graylings have dark transverse spots rather
like the parr marks of salmonids.

The grayling grows to between 25 and 50 cm
(10 to 20 in.) in length. The heaviest recorded

British specimen is said to be one found dead near Shrewsbury and to have weighed 2·268 kg (5 lb). The British rod-caught record for grayling is open at 3 lb (1·360 kg). It is a short-lived fish, most reaching an age of 5 or 6 years, although they have been known to reach 13 or more.

The grayling spawns from March to May and in this respect it is unlike the game fish proper, which are members of the salmon family and spawn in the autumn, winter or early spring. In its breeding season the grayling associates itself with the coarse fish. To the fly fisherman the graylings' spawning season is a very attractive characteristic because he may fish for them when trout are out of season. Because of the different breeding times, trout and grayling do not compete for spawning sites.

The males take up territories in the spawning places in the rivers, and they guard these shallow areas of gravel from rivals. The females push themselves into the gravel, and the eggs are released and fertilised under the gravel surface. The eggs are smaller than those of trout, and from one thousand to thirty thousand are laid, depending on the size of the female.

The food of grayling consists of bottom invertebrates, such as freshwater shrimps, snails, worms and the larvae of caddis and other insects, as well as fish spawn. Small grayling eat flying insects, and jump well clear of the water to catch them. At the times of the emergence of mayflies the grayling feed heavily on them at the surface.

Large specimens eat small fish and there are records of grayling devouring shrews and small rodents crossing the river.

There has been considerable controversy over the extent of the competition for food between grayling and trout. A clue to one aspect of this is the distinct difference in the mouths of the two species; trout have very large mouths with sharp teeth, and the grayling has a very small mouth with smaller teeth. The larger animals with solid shells are crushed by the grayling's powerful stomach muscles. In Sweden it was noticed that there was little competition for food between trout and grayling, but in other places it has been found that if grayling are introduced, the resident trout suffer. The competition is said to reach a situation where the trout dominate the swifter flowing sections of a stream, and the grayling the slower parts.

Grayling inhabit rivers and fast flowing streams, and they like areas where the gradient is not as steep as that of some trout streams, and in which there are pools separating the rapids. The grayling likes well-oxygenated water, but is more tolerant than the trout in this respect. Compared with a typical trout stream, the grayling river has a slightly finer material on the bottom with some gravel and stones, and with the water temperature generally higher. In the northern part of their range, for example in Sweden and Russia, they are found in lakes and quite exceptionally live in brackish water.

The grayling is found throughout Europe from Scandinavia, Finland and Russia, through Germany, Denmark and Switzerland to northern Italy. They are absent in southern Italy, southern France, Spain and Ireland. Within their range they are found in isolated and rather special localities, but when they are present, they are often very plentiful.

In Britain the grayling is found scattered in such rivers as the Severn, Avon, Itchen, Test, Ouse, and Eden. In Scotland they are present in the rivers Nith, Tweed and South Esk.

The grayling is reared artificially in hatcheries in this country and on the continent. A dwarf race (Plate 12) is sometimes found. The scientific name *thymallus* refers to the smell of thyme, and the English name refers to the general colour of the upper parts.

The Smelt

Family OSMERIDAE   *Osmerus eperlanus*

The smelt (Plate 6), like the salmonids, the whitefish and grayling, has an adipose fin and is a member of the sub-order Salmonoidea. Like many of this group it lives in the sea and enters fresh water to spawn, and as with the salmon, trout, whitefish and char, there are some lakes

72

which contain land-locked varieties, but these do not occur in Britain.

The smelt is a small fish, usually about 20 cm (8 in.) in length and rarely exceeding 30 cm (12 in.), although they do grow to 40 cm (16 in.). The body is slender with the greatest depth just in front of the dorsal fin. The lower jaw projects slightly beyond the snout. The mouth and teeth are large, and this gives the fish a rather predatory appearance. The fins are angular and the tail is markedly forked. The lateral line does not extend far down the sides of the body from the head.

The upper parts are green or blue grey-green, the sides are silvery and the belly is white, and the skin of living fish appears semi-transparent. The smelt has a very characteristic and strong smell of cucumbers.

Smelts enter fresh water from February to April to spawn. They ascend the rivers no further than the first rapids, and most of the spawning takes place in the lower reaches. The eggs are heavier than water and are very sticky. They settle on weed, pier piles and stones, to which they remain attached while the embryo develops. The eggs are yellowish, about 1·2 mm in diameter, and a large female may lay up to 40,000. After the eggs have hatched the fry are carried fairly quickly to brackish water. The growth is rapid and smelts mature when two years old.

The food of the fry consists of very small

drifting animals such as larvae of crustacea, copepods and other plankton. The larger smelts eat shrimps, sand-hoppers, marine worms and small fish.

The smelt is a coastal and estuarine fish rather than one of the open sea. The fish are distributed from northern Spain, through the Bay of Biscay and the North Sea to southern Norway and the Baltic. They have been recorded from Iceland and Greenland and are represented by a different, but very similar species on the Atlantic coast of Canada. In Britain smelts are present in the fens, East Anglia, South Yorkshire, the coast of Lancashire, the Shannon and a few other scattered localities.

The smelt is said to be extremely good to eat, fried in deep fat after being dipped in egg and seasoned breadcrumbs. Where they are abundant, they are caught in enormous quantities, not only for human food, but also for making into cattle feed and fertiliser. In these areas they are of very considerable commercial importance.

The Pike

Family ESOCIDAE   *Esox lucius*

The pike (Plate 13) is a very common fish and is probably best known as the most voracious fish-eating carnivore among all the British freshwater species. One glance at the huge mouth with large backward-pointing teeth is enough to convince anyone that we are now dealing with a creature that is well adapted to seizing and swallowing other fish as food.

The pike is a native British fish which is always found in fresh water in this country, although elsewhere, for example in the Baltic, pike have been reported from brackish water which they visit to spawn. Our pike tend to be sluggish fish which remain resident in their particular domains without indulging in any extensive migrations.

Pike grow to a large size, and they have probably led to more fishermen's tales of exaggerated monsters than any other fish. It is very difficult to find the record pike weight. The British rod-caught record is open at 41 lb (18·597 kg), because the National Anglers' Council reconsidered older claims and decided they would have to start a recording system on a more certain basis. Larger pike have been caught in nets or when lakes have been drained. Tate Regan gives details of a 52 lb pike, 4 ft 4 in. long (23·587 kg, 132 cm), obtained in Whittlesea Mere when it was drained in 1851, and other information on the head of a pike from Loch Ken which he estimated could have been 72 lb (32·659 kg) if in good condition. One problem in giving the records in terms of weight is that this can be reduced by a fifth when the female sheds her eggs at spawning time. An outstanding specimen of 65 kg (143 lb) has been recorded from the lower Dnieper in Russia. Most of the record fish have been females since they grow faster and larger than the males. In Windermere in the Lake District a 10 year old male may be 72 cm (28 in.) in length and females of the same age average 92 cm (36 in.). Pike can live to an age of 17 years or more. The scales and the opercular bones both show growth rings from which the age can be determined.

The pike has a very large head with an elongated and flattened snout, like a duck's bill. The body is long and cylindrical with the dorsal fin far back near the tail and vertically above the anal fin. The pelvic fins are also far back. The body is covered with relatively small scales. The pike is olive green or greenish brown on the upper parts and sides, with cream blotches which sometimes appear as diagonal stripes. The undersides are creamy white and the fins are reddish yellow with brown markings. The gill covers and eyes are large.

The pike is mainly an inhabitant of still and slowly moving waters in the lowlands of Britain. Although found in some lakes such as Windermere, it is not common in the peaty or clear highland waters or in fast-flowing upland rivers. It is typically a fish of canals, lazy rivers and meres, with reed beds and plenty of weed.

Pike breed in April or May and they first spawn when they are two or three years old. The female lays between 20 and 35 eggs per gram of her total body weight. The pairs congregate in weedy areas and the eggs and milt are shed together, and after fertilisation the eggs are slightly adhesive and stick to the weeds. The eggs hatch in two or three weeks, depending on the water temperature, and the larval fish have an adhesive organ by which they also stick to the weed. They have a large yolk sac and remain hanging on the weeds and grow by utilising the food reserves in the yolk. After about five days the fry free themselves, swim away and begin to feed on small insects, crustacea and other plankton.

After the fry have grown to 3 cm in length (just over an inch), they begin to feed on fish such as larval perch, minnows and on stickle-backs. The pike will only feed on living animals and from this small size they remain almost entirely fish eaters for the rest of their lives, and they will eat almost any available fish species including their own. They also eat frogs, toads, newts, ducks and other birds, and all kinds of small aquatic mammals.

The ferocity of pike is well known and their reputation deserved. They have been known to consume fish of about their own size and take a considerable time over its digestion. There have also been reports of pike attacking humans, but these are extremely rare. A pike feeds by lying motionless in wait for its prey which it snatches in one great strike. If it misses it waits again and there is never a wild chase hither and thither.

Pike are distributed over most of Britain except the north of Scotland, Cornwall and western Wales, in any reasonable size of pond, canal, river, lake, flooded quarry or similar habitat. Elsewhere the pike is found throughout Europe from the Black Sea and central Italy (but not Spain) to northern Finland (but not Norway), and it is found in northern and western Asia throughout virtually the whole of the Soviet Union. It is present in North America from Alaska to Ohio.

The Carp Family

Family CYPRINIDAE

The cyprinids form a very large and important family of fish, and its members are widely distributed over nearly the whole world. They are mainly freshwater species but some venture into brackish water in localities such as the Baltic.

The cyprinids have the pelvic fins well back along the body, nearly halfway between the snout and the tail, they have no adipose fin, and the jaws are toothless. They are distinguishable from the herring family by not having pointed scales along a keeled belly. However, the main feature of the cyprinids is that they have a pair of special bones in the throat. These bones are called the pharyngeal bones, and they have hard lumps on finger-like processes which can be made to press against a plate connected to the base of the skull. These fish have no teeth in the mouth, but do their chewing down in the throat.

The cyprinids are not always easy to identify, and even two such common species as the roach and the rudd may be difficult to separate, particularly since they interbreed. The goldfish is another cyprinid which is sometimes easy to identify but if it has reverted to its natural coloration it is difficult and requires an expert to confirm the identification. Nevertheless a count of the fin rays and the scales should enable every serious naturalist interested in fish to identify nearly all his specimens. The shape of the pharyngeal bones varies in the different species and so provides the easiest method for certain identification, but this requires dissecting them and so the specimen has to be dead. A description of the pharyngeal bones is outside the scope of this book, and if it is necessary to examine them, the general naturalist should call in the expert.

The cyprinids can be divided into three principal groups as follows:

Group I Dorsal fin long, with 14 to 23 branched rays: carp, crucian carp, goldfish

Group II Dorsal fin short with less than 14 branched rays and anal fin also short with 13 or less branched rays: barbel, gudgeon, tench, minnow, chub, dace, roach and rudd

Group III Dorsal fin short with less than 14
branched rays and anal fin long with
15 to 29 branched rays: white bream,
common bream and bleak.

The Common Carp

Family CYPRINIDAE   *Cyprinus carpio*

The common carp (Plate 14) was not originally
a native British fish, but it has now been completely naturalised for many centuries. In this
country it is only important as a sport fish for
anglers, but throughout much of Europe and the
Middle East it is an extremely important commercially bred fish which is grown in very large
numbers in ponds for food. The carp is said
to have been kept for food in monastery ponds
to provide fish on meatless days. Like many
other domesticated animals which have been
subjected to selective breeding, the carp has
several different varieties, namely the mirror carp,
leather carp and king carp. These will be
discussed later.

The colour of the carp is very variable, ranging
from muddy slate to blue-green or brownish
green on the upper parts with the sides blue-
green, golden yellow or straw coloured. The
underparts vary from orange or yellow to buff or
white. The scales are large and have a metallic
sheen; the back of each scale is outlined with
black pigment. The fins are dark blue-green

and the tail fin is tinted with red or pink. The dorsal fin is long with 3 or 4 unbranched rays followed by 16 to 22 branched rays, and this fin has a concave upper surface. It commences halfway along the rather humped back and extends nearly to the tail. The body is a fat oval in section, giving the fish a slightly bloated appearance when seen from the front. The mouth is at the end of the snout and the lips are thick and leathery. The common carp is distinguishable from the crucian carp and goldfish by having two short barbels at each side of the mouth and a strongly forked tail fin.

The carp can grow to a large size. The British rod-caught record stands at 44 lb (19·958 kg) taken at Redmire Pool in 1952, but most carp in Britain are 4 to 7 lb (1·8 to 3·2 kg), or exceptionally up to 15 lb (6·8 kg). However, the cultivated varieties regularly grow to a size of 60 lb (27 kg) or more and have a pronounced humped back.

Carp prefer the warmer water in the south of England, and like weedy lakes, ponds or slow-flowing rivers and canals.

The species is essentially a bottom feeder and it eats all kinds of animals and plants which are crushed with the broad flat surfaces on the pharyngeal bones. The carp roots down to a depth of 10 to 13 cm (4 to 5 in.) into the mud, and sucks up mud along with more nutritious material. The mud passes right through the alimentary canal and the food material is digested and absorbed.

Spawning takes place in shallow water from May to July. The males develop tubercles on the head and pectoral fins. The eggs are sticky and are deposited on the leaves of aquatic plants. They are transparent and about 1·5 mm in diameter. The fecundity of the female is enormous and is reported to range up to 150,000 per pound of body weight. Like the pike, the carp larva has an adhesive organ by means of which it sticks to the plant leaves for a day or two.

Carp originate from the region of the Black Sea and Caspian, and from the large area between Burma and the Russian–Chinese border. In Europe carp are found from southern Sweden and Scotland southwards to France, Spain, Italy, Greece and Israel. In Britain they are found in the scattered localities where they have been introduced mainly south of a line from York to Preston.

In Britain, and indeed over most of its range, the carp is a sedentary resident, but in some places, for example in the Volga delta, it migrates to the sea.

The varieties of carp arise from their artificial selection through domestication. The variation takes the form of a loss of scales, which makes their preparation for the table easier and more pleasant. Their growth rate has also been considerably increased. In the mirror carp there are patches on the body which lack scales completely. The scales that are present are usually found along the base of the dorsal fin and sometimes along the lateral line and may be scattered elsewhere. Mirror carp are essentially semi-scaleless fish, but the leather carp has gone a stage further, and is almost completely devoid of scales and is covered with a tough skin. A few degenerate scales are usually present by the dorsal fin or the tail. Although these varieties are popular in the kitchen, they are not as hardy as the fully scaled carp, and if left to their own devices they revert in a few generations to fully scaled fish which are called king carp. These are feral carp and are very difficult to distinguish from true wild carp though they differ in growth rate and in uneven scaling. The golden carp is a fish of ornamental ponds, and it is an ordinary carp lacking the normal pigmentation. Its lack of camouflage would not render its survival likely in the wild.

The Crucian Carp

Family CYPRINIDAE   *Carassius carassius*

The crucian carp (Plate 15), like the common carp, is not a native of Britain, but originally came from Asia. It has now spread, or has been spread by anglers, over a wide area. It is thought to have been introduced later than the common carp, perhaps in the seventeenth century. The crucian carp is a resident wherever it has established itself, and does not indulge in any extensive migrations.

Like the common carp, the crucian has been domesticated in commercial ponds, but this has not led to scaleless varieties. It is not so popular as a food fish, even though it grows quickly, because it is smaller. The British rod-caught record stands at 4 lb 15½ oz (2·253 kg). They can grow up to 50 cm (20 in.) and 5 kg (11 lb) in weight.

The common and crucian carps are similar in having a long dorsal fin extending from about halfway along the back nearly to the tail, but in the crucian the dorsal fin is rounded on the top edge. The number of rays in this fin is 3 or 4 unbranched and 14 to 21 branched, so that this feature cannot be used for identifying the species. The body is hump-backed. The upper parts are a dark olive or brown-green and the sides are a metallic yellow or red. There is often a dark spot in front of the tail fin. The belly is buff or cream.

The habitat of the crucian carp comprises stagnant or slowly flowing water, whether this is in sluggish rivers, canals, ponds, lakes or gravel pits. In these situations the crucian carp likes plenty of rooted vegetation and other weed.

Breeding takes place intermittently in May and June and the eggs are laid on the leaves of aquatic plants. Crucian carp feed on small animals and on vegetable matter which is obtained by rooting about on the bottom, in which operation a great deal of indigestible mud is consumed.

The distribution of this species is mainly in the southern and eastern parts of England, particularly in East Anglia, Hampshire and Sussex. They have not been recorded from Ireland or Scotland. They are distributed over most of central and eastern Europe from southern France, Italy and Sicily to southern Finland, but they are not found in southern and western France or Switzerland. They do not extend into central Asia.

The crucian carp is very tenacious of life and it is said to remain alive in mud even when the pond it is in is almost dry, and it is more satisfactory to transport these fish in wet newspaper than in a can in which they might get bruised.

Hybrids are encountered wherever the common carp and crucian carp occur together, but as a rule they are sterile.

The Goldfish

Family CYPRINIDAE   *Carassius auratus*

The goldfish must surely be the best known fish imported into Britain. The number given away in polythene bags at fairs, testifies to the hardiness and ease of transport of this species. Although it is so widely known, not all brightly coloured fish are goldfish, and not all goldfish are brightly coloured, so there are many possibilities of confusion for the unwary.

85

Goldfish originated from southern Manchuria, China, Japan, Korea and Formosa, and they arrived in this country in 1691. After the first importations, enormous numbers must have been brought in and bred although the art of breeding exotic and brightly coloured specimens has been most highly perfected in China and Japan.

The colour of the cultivated goldfish ranges from red, through orange to yellow, with white or black patches, and particular attention has been paid to breeding exotic fin forms. The original colours are very much drabber, being an olive-green or brown on the back, shading through bronze to off-white or buff below. With this coloration they are very similar to the common and crucian carps. They can be distinguished from common carp by the lack of barbels, and from crucian carp by the lack of a black spot near the tail, larger scales and a more concave dorsal fin (like that of the common carp). Also the first spine of the goldfish's dorsal fin has a serrated edge and feels rough. Wild goldfish are very difficult to identify with any certainty, and if a wild fish is suspected of being of this species, it should definitely be sent to an expert for examination.

Goldfish in ornamental ponds can grow to a considerable size, but those in nature are usually only 15 to 30 cm (6 to 12 in.) long. They are usually found in ponds and small lakes, and hardly ever in flowing waters. Very little appears to be known about the food and breeding habits of wild goldfish in Britain, other than that they are probably similar to those of the crucian carp.

The distribution of the goldfish in Britain is very scattered and is related to where they have been introduced.

The goldfish is a very hardy fish and thrives well in ornamental ponds in this country; like the crucian carp it is very tenacious of life. The brightly coloured cultivated specimens are unlikely to avoid the attentions of predators if liberated into the natural environment.

The Barbel

Family CYPRINIDAE   *Barbus barbus*

The barbel (Plate 16) is one of the group of cyprinid fishes having short dorsal and anal fins. It looks like a long drawn out carp with a short dorsal fin.

The barbel is a large fish and it grows up to 90 cm (3 ft) long and 9 kg (20 lb) in weight in this country, and up to 10 kg (22 lb) on the Continent. The British rod-caught record stands at 13 lb 12 oz (6.237 kg).

The feature that one notices first in the barbel is the presence of four long barbels which give it its name. These hang down from near the mouth which is under the long snout, and they are almost equal in length. The short dorsal fin has only eight or nine branched rays. The body is long and cylindrical, only becoming flattened at the tail; the head is flattened from above. The lips are fleshy and thick. The tail fin is deeply forked with the top lobe being pointed and the lower lobe slightly rounded. The colour of the upper parts is very variable, ranging from olive-green and grey-green to dark slate coloured. The sides are paler and the belly is a pearly white. The fins are grey-green with red towards the tips of the paired fins and with reddish streaks on the tail fin. The body and fins sometimes have small brown spots.

Large numbers of barbel spawn together in sandy and stony places from May to mid-June after a migration up-stream to the smaller and shallower tributaries. The ripe males develop rows of white tubercles on the head and back. The eggs, which are yellowish, 2 mm in diameter, adhere to the stones and gravel. The roe, as well as the eggs, is said to be poisonous. The food of the barbel is mainly animal in origin, consisting of insects, worms, fish eggs, and snails and bivalve molluscs.

The barbel is a gregarious fish and lives in shoals in swift-flowing, stony and well-oxygenated rivers with plenty of vegetation, seeking food by night and congregating in deep pools by day. The barbel in England is not found north of Yorkshire, but is present in Hampshire, the Thames basin, the Severn, the Yorkshire Ouse and elsewhere. It is not found in Ireland or Scotland. In Europe it is distributed throughout

Germany, Holland, Belgium, France, northern
Italy and Dalmatia, but not in Scandinavia.

The Gudgeon

Family CYPRINIDAE   *Gobio gobio*

The gudgeon (Plate 17) is a smaller version of the
barbel with only two barbels instead of four.
Most specimens are only 12 to 15 cm (5 to 6 in.)
in length, even when fully grown, and the British
rod-caught record is at 4 oz (113 g).   In Europe
they have been known to reach 20 cm (8 in.) in
length.

The back is grey or brown with a greenish
tint, the sides are yellowish and the belly is
silvery with a reddish iridescence.   The body
has a row of 6 to 10 dark spots about the same
size as the eye along each side.   There are also
other light and dark spots and speckles scattered
over the body.   The dorsal and tail fins are
grey-yellow with rows of dark brown speckles,
and the other fins are colourless.   The tail is
distinctly forked.

The gudgeon can be distinguished from the
ruffe by the form of the dorsal fin which does not
have any spines as the first fin rays.   It differs
from the loaches in its more pronounced taper
from the dorsal fin to the tail, more deeply divided
tail fin, and in its only having two barbels.   This
latter feature distinguishes it from small barbel.
The cylindrical body is thickest in front of the

dorsal fin and tapers rapidly to the tail. The head is wedge shaped and the mouth with the two barbels is under the snout.

The gudgeon is a bottom living fish, mainly of swift-flowing rivers, but also on lake shores. It is mostly found where the bottom is stony and gravelly. In these localities the gudgeon is gregarious and large shoals may sometimes be seen on the bottom, but they tend to be mainly in the deeper and darker pools.

Spawning takes place in May and June in running water. The eggs are sticky and adhere in clumps to the stones and gravel, and also sometimes to weeds. The eggs are liberated in batches a few at a time. Incubation takes about ten days and the young hatch with a large yolk sac.

Gudgeon feed on bottom-living animals such as mayfly nymphs, caddis larvae, midge larvae, freshwater shrimps and worms, as well as some vegetable matter.

Gudgeon are found throughout much of Britain, but not in Cornwall and only very rarely north of Yorkshire. It is present in Ireland. In Europe it is absent from Spain, central Italy, and Greece, but is distributed through central Europe, but not in northern Scandinavia. It extends through eastern Europe and parts of Asia to China.

This unfortunate fish is often used as live bait, but it does not receive much other attention from anglers, apart from schoolboys.

The Tench

Family CYPRINIDAE   *Tinca tinca*

When seen in pond or aquarium, the tench seems a large, lethargic slimy kind of fish, but like many such animals it has considerable strength (Plate 18).

Tench are usually 20 to 30 cm long (8 to 12 in.), but they sometimes grow to over 50 cm (20 in.). The British rod-caught record stands at 9 lb 1 oz (4·11 kg) for a fish caught in 1963 at Hemingford Grey. One tench from Kiev in 1857 is reported to have weighed 7·5 kg (16½ lb).

The body of the tench is thickset and stocky, with a large tail and rounded fins. The mouth is at the end of the smallish head and has two small barbels. The scales are small and deeply embedded in the thick slimy skin. Tench from muddy water tend to be dark brownish olive-green, or almost black, but those from clearer or running water are a pale olive or light green. The flanks and belly are paler than the back and are bronze or greenish yellow with a golden sheen. The fins are always dark grey or black, large and rounded with thick fin rays. The tench is unlikely to be confused with any other fish.

Tench are fish of very weedy, still or flowing water with a muddy bottom. As well as such waters, typified by the Norfolk Broads, tench thrive in any small lake or pond provided there is sufficient mud, and also weed to give shelter from predators. The oxygen requirements of tench are very low indeed, even when compared with perch and roach, and this means that they can thrive in stagnant waters and root around in the deeper parts which are almost de-oxygenated.

Tench breed very late in the year, from mid-May to the latter half of July. It is said that spawning takes place after thunderstorms. The tench congregate in shoals, and the eggs, which are 1·2 mm in diameter, are laid amongst plants, and become stuck to the leaves. They are said to hatch out in about a week to give very small larvae. The adults mature when three, or occasionally two, years of age. They live to an age of ten years or more. The fecundity is enormous and an individual can lay 800,000 eggs.

The food of tench consists of animals such as midge larvae and worms which are obtained by rooting in the bottom mud, and tench penetrate some 7 cm (almost 3 in.) into the bottom. With this type of feeding a considerable quantity of mud, sand, and dead animal and plant material is also swallowed, and the indigestible parts pass right through the fish. In this way the tench helps to keep the pond clean and prevent the accumulation of decaying material in stagnant waters. Tench also feed on molluscs which are picked off the leaves of aquatic plants.

Tench are distributed widely south of a line from York to Preston. In Europe they are present from Sicily in the south to southern Norway, Sweden and Finland in the north.

Tench are very tenacious of life and survive in the mud of dried-up ponds, and can be transported easily in wet newspaper. It used to be thought that the slime of tench had medicinal properties, and so it was called the 'doctor fish'!

In Britain the tench is much sought after by anglers. On the Continent it is cultivated in fish ponds, where its firm, well-flavoured flesh is appreciated.

One variety, the golden tench, is a semi-albino form and is a very beautiful fish which is kept in ornamental ponds.

The Minnow

Family CYPRINIDAE   *Phoxinus phoxinus*

The minnow (Plate 19) is one of the commonest and best-known small British fish, and it is often found in large numbers in a shoal.

In Britain minnows rarely exceed 10 cm (4 in.), but specimens of 12·5 cm (5 in.) have been recorded. They live to an age of five years. The head is blunt and the body cylindrical and thickest at the front, with a very marked lateral thinning towards the tail. The lateral line is often missing in parts along its length. The short dorsal fin is set relatively far back and the tail fin is large and widely forked. The scales are minute and there are 80 to 90 along the lateral line.

The minnow is a handsome fish and is unlikely to be confused with any other species. The ground colour of the back is usually grey-green, and the flanks are paler shading to silvery below. Along the sides of the body are irregular darker spots or vertical stripes, but the arrangement of these and their nearness to each other, often makes them appear more conspicuously as a horizontal band from the tip of the snout to the tail, and this appearance is often accentuated by a horizontal golden or yellow band as well. The underparts are white or silvery, tinted with pink. The rounded fins are yellowish.

Minnows prefer the well-oxygenated water of fast-flowing streams and rivers, or cooler lakes with clear water, and they are unable to prosper in stagnant pools or ditches. They will leap out of a badly aerated aquarium, and this is the fate of many specimens that result from children's fishing excursions.

Minnows breed from March to June. They congregate in large numbers in shallow places with clean gravel and sand. Here the eggs are deposited and stick to the stones. Each female may lay from 100 to 600 eggs. At spawning time the males develop horny white tubercles on the head, and a red colour appears at the corners of the mouth, round the gills and on the belly. The minnows in lakes either spawn among the gravel near the shore, or migrate to spawn in the inflowing streams.

Minnows feed largely on midge larvae, and also on planktonic crustacea and other small animals as well as on a certain amount of vegetable matter.

This species is widespread throughout Britain, but is not present in the north of Scotland. In Ireland it is less common and its distribution is very local. Minnows are found through Europe and Asia from Spain to the Russian–Manchurian border. They do not occur in central or southern Italy or southern Balkans or in Iceland. In the Baltic, and probably elsewhere, minnows are found in brackish water.

The flesh of minnows is said to be excellent, but in Britain this fish is rarely, if ever, used for human food. On the Continent and in Russia there is a regular fishery for them.

Minnows fall prey to many natural predators, including trout, perch and above all, pike, which is why they are often unfortunately used as live bait.

The Orfe

Family CYPRINIDAE   *Leuciscus idus*

The situation in this country with the orfe, or ide as it is sometimes called, parallels that of the goldfish. It is not a native British species, but varieties have been imported into this country for stocking ornamental ponds, and from these they have escaped, or been liberated, and they have reverted to their natural coloration. Also like the feral goldfish wild orfe are extremely difficult to identify with certainty and the expert must be consulted.

The body is slightly hump-backed and laterally compressed, but the orfe is a very graceful fish. It grows from 30 to 50 cm (12 to 20 in.). The British rod-caught record is 3 lb 14½ oz (1·772 kg). On the Continent specimens of 1 m (40 in.) and 6 to 8 kg (13½ to 17½ lb) have been recorded. The colour of wild orfe is dark greyish green or blue above the lateral line with paler sides below, and a silvery belly. The dorsal and tail fins are greyish, and the paired fins and the anal fin, are reddish. The tail is well forked.

Orfe inhabit sluggish rivers and deep lakes.

Spawning takes place from April to June and the large eggs, which are 2·2 mm in diameter, are laid on stones and plants with much commotion and splashing inshore.

Orfe feed on insect larvae, mayflies and other adult insects, worms, fish spawn, molluscs, plankton and crustacea. Orfe are useful in garden ponds because they keep down the numbers of biting mosquitoes.

Feral orfe are very rare, and in Britain the distribution depends on where they have escaped from ornamental ponds. In Europe they are found from central France to central Finland and Sweden, but only in south-eastern Norway, and they go into brackish water in the upper parts of the Baltic. This is an important commercial fish, particularly in eastern Europe and Russia.

The golden orfe of ornamental ponds is golden on the back and silvery below with a rosy tint. It can appear similar to a very slim rudd, and the silver orfe which is greenish blue above and silver below, is like the dace. These fish can be distinguished by the expert on the basis of scale and fin ray counts, and any wild fish suspected of being this species should definitely be preserved and sent to an expert for examination.

The Chub

Family CYPRINIDAE   *Leuciscus cephalus*

The chub (Plate 19) is a fish which is liable to be confused with other species and although its size immediately distinguishes it from some of the smaller kinds, one must remember that all large fish have had to be small at some time in their lives.

Chub grow to a fair size and although this is usually between 30 and 50 cm (12 and 20 in.), they may reach 60 cm (24 in.) in Britain. The British rod-caught record is open at 7 lb (3·175 kg). On the Continent they grow to 80 cm (31 in.) and 4 kg (9 lb). One has been recorded from the Ukraine weighing 8 kg (17$\frac{1}{2}$ lb).

The body of the chub is long and powerful.

The head is large and the mouth big with thick lips. The corner of the mouth often reaches to vertically below the middle of the eye. The edge of the dorsal fin is either straight or slightly convex, and the anal fin is always convex. The tail fin is narrowly forked.

The colour of the back is dark green, greenish grey or brown, or greyish blue. The sides and belly are white or silvery with a metallic bronze or golden sheen. The sides of the head in particular can have a reddish bronze glint. The dorsal and tail fins are dark grey tinged with yellow or red, and the pelvic and anal fins are reddish. The scales are large and dark edged, which accentuates them and gives a cross-hatched appearance.

Small chub can be distinguished from dace by not having a concave dorsal fin; by having a large mouth; by the shorter, less deeply notched tail fin; whereas dace nearly always have more than 47 scales along the lateral line, chub almost certainly have fewer. Confusion need only arise when counting the scales is difficult, or with fish that have exactly 47 along the lateral line. Chub are sometimes referred to as skelly, but can be distinguished from the true whitefish schelly, by not having an adipose fin. Chub can be separated from grey mullet because they have only one dorsal fin, and are not striped or gregarious when adult.

The chub is a species typical of rivers that have a gentle gradient and moderate current, that remain reasonably well oxygenated even at the height of summer, and that are well provided with aquatic vegetation. Although essentially river fish, chub are also recorded from still waters where they feed on the bottom.

Chub breed from April to June when the sticky eggs are deposited on stones, gravel and water weed. Chub are said to spawn in pairs, and not gregariously like many other cyprinids. The eggs hatch in about one week. The males develop tubercles at the breeding season. They mature at about three years of age, and the females at four. Young chub are gregarious, and large shoals may be seen by the lucky naturalist. The older fish become solitary and less active, and are then most often seen swimming lethargically in the same place near some tree roots or weed.

The food of chub consists of insects and other small animals, as well as appreciable amounts of vegetable matter. When older they consume small fish, frogs, crayfish and fish eggs.

Chub are widely distributed in England, but are not found in Cornwall and only rarely in Devon and Wales. In Scotland they are not recorded north of Dumfries. Chub were absent from Ireland until recently, when thriving populations were reported from the River Blackwater. It is likely that these fish will spread elsewhere. On the Continent they are present in northern France, Germany, Switzerland, southern Sweden and Norway, in Finland

and the Danube basin and much of Russia as far as the Ural Mountains, but not in Denmark.

Chub are sought after by anglers and are considered a pest in trout waters, since they are believed to be predators and competitors for food. Chub have a rather tasteless flesh and an incredible number of bones; cooked chub has been said to resemble cotton wool well stuffed with needles.

The Dace

Family CYPRINIDAE   *Leuciscus leuciscus*

The dace (Plate 19) is one of the commonest and most elegant of the British coarse fish. It is small, being usually 20 to 25 cm (8 to 10 in.) in length and only exceptionally up to 30 cm (12 in.). The weight is usually about 200 g (7 oz) but sometimes up to 500 g (1 lb 1¾ oz). The British rod-caught record is open at 1 lb 4½ oz (574 g).

The dace is a very graceful fish, whose body is slim and well streamlined. The mouth is small, slightly below the snout, and the corner of the mouth does not extend as far back as vertically below the eye. The fins are delicate and fan-shaped. The dorsal and anal fins are concave, and the tail fin is deeply forked.

The dace is predominantly silver in colour over the sides, although the back is a steely blue-black or dark olive-blue, and the belly is a cream or white. The dark colour of the back is restricted to a fairly narrow stripe and hardly extends to the sides. The scales, like those of the chub, are dark edged which gives a cross-hatched appearance. The fins are grey or pale yellow.

Dace are river fish and like fast-flowing well-oxygenated water particularly near a weir or where shallows increase the current. Most often the presence of dace is given away by a flash of silver as a fish turns beneath the surface. They are a very gregarious species and do not sulk in the depths but dart about together in the upper waters. They are found in the same type of river as trout, and are found higher than chub. When found in lakes it is nearly always near the inflow or outflow where the current is appreciable. They do not occur naturally where the water is still.

The differences between chub and dace were discussed under the former species. The dace is unlikely to be confused with the roach because it has a thinner and more streamlined body and the fins are grey.

Dace breed from March to May. The eggs are large, about 2 mm in diameter. The male develops tubercles at the breeding season.

Dace feed mainly on animals, such as insect larvae, plankton, adult insects, crustacea, worms and snails, and only rarely on vegetable material. The larvae of caddis, *Simulium* (black fly) and midges are the favourite food of dace along with freshwater shrimps.

Dace are distributed throughout England, but are absent from western Wales and Scotland. They are present in Ireland in the River Blackwater system. They are absent in Spain, Italy and Dalmatia, but present through the rest of Europe including Sweden, Finland and southern Norway. In Russia dace appear to go as far east as the Ural Mountains, beyond which they are replaced by a closely related species.

Dace are a popular sport fish. The flesh is said to be like that of the chub, coarse and bony.

The Roach

Family CYPRINIDAE   *Rutilus rutilus*

The roach (Plate 20) is one of the freshwater fishes best known to anglers. It usually grows to a length of 15 to 30 cm (6 to 12 in.) or even 40 cm (16 in.) and a weight of up to 900 g (2 lb). The British rod-caught record stands at 3 lb 14 oz (1·758 kg).

The body of the roach is laterally flattened and the amount it is hump-backed is very variable; in some localities they are very streamlined whereas elsewhere the older specimens become very much deeper and hump-backed.

The back can be any combination of dark grey, blue and green. The sides are usually silvery with a brassy sheen. The belly is lighter. The dorsal and tail fins are grey-brown, and the others are pink, red or orange. The mouth is small. Roach may easily be confused with rudd, and the distinguishing features are given under that species. The roach interbreeds with the bream, bleak, rudd and silver bream. It is not possible to consider these hybrids here, but if a fish cannot be readily identified as a definite species, it should be sent to an expert for examination.

Roach generally inhabit still or slowly flowing water whether it be in a lake, pond, canal, river, stream or dyke. They do not need as much oxygen as do trout, nor as little as tench. Nevertheless they are able to live in many stagnant waters, but they do not have the capacity to withstand a fast current. They thrive and form large shoals in the intermediate, slowly flowing rivers.

Roach breed when four, or sometimes three, years of age, gregariously together with much noise. The small sticky eggs are laid amongst the leaves of plants. After about 12 days the larvae hatch and remain hanging for a few days from the leaves by an adhesive organ. Then they move to the bank and begin to feed on minute plankton. The spawning season is in May and early June.

The growth rate of roach varies in different localities as is shown below (in centimetres):

| | Age (years) | | | | | | |
---	1	2	3	4	5	6	7
Norfolk Broads	6·9	9·3	11·2	12·7	13·7	15·6	17·5
River Cam	7·0	10·6	13·0	16·2	18·2	21·1	—
Llyn Tegid (Wales)		7·2	10·7	13·5	15·8	17·7	19·5	21·3

The food of roach is also variable from one locality to another. In some places it consists mainly of midge larvae, freshwater shrimps, molluscs, planktonic crustacea and adult insects, and in another locality a large amount of weed may be eaten.

Roach are very widely distributed through Britain as far north as Loch Lomond, but are rare in Devon, Cornwall and western Wales. They used to be absent in Ireland, but are now well established in the rivers Foyle and Mourne, Erne and Blackwater. In the rest of Europe they are present from the Pyrenees to the White Sea and eastwards to Siberia. Brackish water forms are found in the Baltic, Black and Caspian Seas.

The Rudd

Family CYPRINIDAE *Scardinius erythrophthalmus*

The rudd (Plate 20) is very similar indeed to the roach in its external appearance and it is extremely likely that very many mistakes in identification are made between the two species.

The rudd is usually about 20 to 30 cm (8 to 12 in.) in length and 33 cm (13 in.) is a large specimen. The weight is usually around 100 to 300 g (3½ to 10½ oz). The British rod-caught record stands at 4 lb 8 oz (2·041 kg) for a fish caught at Thetford in 1933.

The body of the rudd is laterally flattened, hump-backed and deep, the head is small and the jaw is upturned and the belly keeled between the pelvic and anal fins. The start of the dorsal fin is usually well behind the line vertically above the pelvics. Rudd often are brightly coloured. The back is a dark combination of brown, blue or green and shades to a metallic shining bronze or golden silver on the sides. The belly is white, cream or yellowish. The dorsal fin is often bright red, but can be reddish brown, pink or orange. The anal and tail fins are red with grey bases.

The most certain way of distinguishing between rudd and roach is by examining the pharyngeal bones, which are in two rows in the rudd and one in the roach. However, since their extraction is a matter for the expert, and means killing the fish, the naturalist has to rely on the form of the mouth, which is more upturned in the rudd; the position of the dorsal fin, well behind the level of the pelvics in the rudd and vertically above them in the roach; and the belly scales between the pelvic and the anal fins, which are keeled in the rudd.

The rudd breeds slightly later than the roach, from May to July, when the spawn is deposited on plants in shallow water. The development is similar to that of the roach. The food of the rudd is also similar to that of the roach, with perhaps more vegetable matter, which in the Norfold Broads may account for $\frac{3}{4}$ of their diet. They do not feed on the bottom, but often take adult insects from the surface.

The rudd is not so widely distributed as the

roach and there is only one record from Scotland, but it has been known from Ireland for a long time. In Europe rudd extend from northern Italy and southern France into southern Scandinavia and the Gulf of Finland. It is not found in Greece or Spain and spreads eastwards as far as the Ural Mountains.

The Common Bream

Family CYPRINIDAE   *Abramis brama*

The two British breams are the most hump-backed of our freshwater fishes and they form the group of cyprinids which have long anal fins.

The common bream (Plate 21) is usually between 30 and 45 cm long (12 and 18 in.), but may grow to 75 cm (29½ in.) and 6 kg (13 lb). The British rod-caught record is at 12 lb 14 oz (5·840 kg). In July 1912 a common bream of 11·55 kg (25½ lb) was caught in Finland.

The common bream is very flattened laterally and it has a very deep and hump-backed body with the short dorsal fin starting behind the top of the hump. The head is relatively small. The long anal fin has 3 unbranched rays and 23 to 30 branched ones. The tail fin is deeply forked with the upper lobe pointed and the lower one rounded. In spite of being well scaled, the bream is a very slimy fish.

The colour of the common bream is a dark grey or black with a marked green tinge. The sides are a paler green-brown with a metallic sheen.

The belly is white or cream. The fins are grey and can have black tips.

The common bream is found in large shoals in slowly flowing or stagnant lakes, ponds and canals. Bream can survive the very low oxygen concentrations found in these waters in summer.

The spawning season is from May to July. The males, which develop tubercles on the body and fins, defend territories of some 5 m (16 ft approx.) with much splashing, and the females pair with them. The sticky yellow eggs of 1·5 mm diameter are deposited on the leaves of weeds.

The food of bream contains much planktonic crustacea, water fleas, and also midge larvae for larger fish, and molluscs only for those of 18 cm (7 in.) or over.

The common bream is found through most of lowland Britain, particularly in the south and east. It is absent in Scotland north of Dumfries, the west country, western Wales and north-east England. It is common in Ireland. In Europe it is present from the Pyrenees and Alps northwards to the White Sea. In the Baltic, Black Sea and Sea of Azov bream live in brackish water.

The White Bream

Family CYPRINIDAE   *Blicca bjoerkna*

The white (or silver) bream (Plate 22) is superficially like a small common bream and the young of the latter are probably often mistaken for the white bream and vice versa. The usual size of adult white bream is 15 to 20 cm (6 to 8 in.) up to 30 cm (12 in.), and the weight is usually about 450 g (1 lb), but up to 2·04 kg (4½ lb) has been recorded. The British rod-caught record is open at 1½ lb (680 g).

The body of the white bream is very flat laterally and hump-backed and slimy. The top of the head and back are grey or brown-olive-green, and the flanks, belly and sides of the head are silvery. The dorsal, tail and anal fins are dark grey and the paired fins are lighter with red or pink at their bases.

The white bream can usually be distinguished from the common bream by counting the anal fin rays, which in this species are 3 unbranched and 19 to 23 branched, compared with 3 unbranched and 23 to 28 branched in the common bream. In the dorsal fin both species have 3 unbranched rays, and there are 8 branched in the white, and 9 in the common, bream. The pharyngeal teeth of the white bream are in two rows and only one in the common bream, but since this identification feature involves killing the fish and removing the bones, it is more suited to the zoologist than the general naturalist.

The habitat of the white bream is still or slowly flowing waters with usually much weed. The fish breed in May or June when the pale yellow eggs, 2 mm in diameter, are attached to submerged leaves. Apparently the eggs are shed in two or more batches.

The food is very similar to that of the common bream, and consists of water fleas, much plant material, some insects and snails.

The white bream is restricted in Britain to the east of England from Essex to Yorkshire, including Lincolnshire, Nottinghamshire, Cambridgeshire, and the Norfolk Broads with a few records from the Midlands, Cheshire, South Devon and elsewhere. In Europe they extend through central France to southern Scandinavia (and the Gulf of Finland) and eastwards to the rivers flowing into the Caspian.

The Bleak

Family CYPRINIDAE   *Alburnus alburnus*

The bleak (Plate 22) is a small cyprinid with a short dorsal fin, long anal fin and a slim spindle-shaped body. The mouth is small and upturned. The pectoral fins are close to the gill covers, and the pectorals are in front of the line from the dorsal fin. The tail fin is well forked. The scales are easily detached.

The size of adult bleak is from about 10 to 15 cm (4 to 6 in.) and only rarely above 20 cm (8 in.). The British rod-caught record stands at 3 oz 15 drms (111 g) for a fish caught near Newark in Nottinghamshire. The back is blue or grey-green, and the sides and belly are silvery. The fins are grey, sometimes tinted with pink.

The bleak is a lively shoaling fish living near the surface of large and small rivers, lakes and ponds. It is often seen close to the bank or splashing at the surface. In the Russian River Don, they are said to form shoals of 8 to 10 million fish with a total weight of over 30 tons.

Bleak spawn intermittently from April into July in shallow gravelly places. The eggs, which are 1·6 mm in diameter, adhere firmly to the stones.

Bleak feed almost entirely on plankton—the small mid-water drifting crustacea—but they also eat any flying insects that may happen to fall on the surface.

This species is not found in England north of Yorkshire or in Ireland, western Wales or Scotland. It is present throughout France and as far north as southern Scandinavia, and as far east as the Ural Mountains.

Bleak are used in the manufacture of artificial pearls. The silvery material is scraped from the scales, preserved and mixed with wax, and the best quality pearls are hollow glass beads filled with this mixture. Poorer pearls are solid beads coated with the silvery material. The discovery of these processes is said to have been made by a rosary manufacturer in about 1656. Since then enormous numbers have been slaughtered for this industry since it is said that the scales from 18,000 bleak are needed to make 1 lb of the extract.

Bleak hybridise with chub and roach and any suspected hybrids should be preserved and sent to an expert for examination.

The Bitterling

Family CYPRINIDAE   *Rhodeus sericeus*

This is not a native British fish but has recently become naturalised in parts of Cheshire, Shropshire, Lancashire and possibly elsewhere.

The bitterling (Plate 23) is a small fish, usually of 4 to 7 cm (1½ to 2¾ in.) or exceptionally 9 cm (3½ in.). The body is hump-backed and flattened laterally. The lateral line does not extend completely beyond the first 5 or 6 scales. The colour of the back is grey-green or grey-blue with the sides and belly silvery with blue iridescent streaks. The fins are red or pink with grey streaks. During the breeding season the males develop a multicoloured iridescence and the fins become brighter.

Bitterling feed on all kinds of small animals and some plant material. The breeding of the bitterling is very peculiar. The eggs (which are oval) pass down a tube into the exhalant breathing siphon of a freshwater mussel. The male bitterling sheds milt over the mussel, whose breathing current then draws the sperm over the eggs which are fertilised and develop inside the mussel. After hatching and some growth, they leave the mussel and seek the shelter of weeds. The female moves on to another mussel, so spawning takes some time and extends from March to August.

In Europe bitterling are found from France,

eastwards to Asia. They are not present in Spain, Italy, Denmark or Scandinavia.

The Stone Loach

Family COBITIDAE   *Noemacheilus barbatulus*

The loaches belong to a small group related to the carp family from which they can be distinguished by having at least six barbels, as well as by anatomical characters which need not concern us here.

The stone loach (Plate 17) is a small elongated fish with one short dorsal, and one short anal fin, and two long and four shorter barbels. The head is flattened and the fins are angular. The tail fin is square or only slightly rounded. The scales are minute and do not overlap. The colour of the back is a dark olive or blue-black and the sides are buff, and the whole of the body is covered with irregular brownish spots. The dorsal and tail fins have rows of dark speckles.

The stone loach is usually 10 to 13 cm (4 to $5\frac{1}{4}$ in.) in length, but occasionally up to 19 cm ($7\frac{1}{2}$ in.). The life-span is three to five years.

This species hides under stones in clear streams and rivers with pure water, and on the shores of lakes. The stone loach nearly always lives in well-oxygenated water, although it is able to supplement the oxygen supply by rising to the surface and swallowing air. This air passes through the intestines, and later bubbles issue from the anus. An analysis of the air taken in and that released shows that oxygen is abstracted and carbon dioxide added, and this indicates that the air supplements the oxygen obtained through the gills from the water. The frequency of swallowing air increases when the water becomes more deficient of oxygen.

Stone loach breed in April and May when the eggs are stuck to the undersides of stones. At this time tubercles appear in both sexes on the insides of the pectoral fins.

Stone loach feed on small bottom invertebrates of all kinds, including insects, freshwater shrimps and also fish eggs.

This species is distributed through most of the British Isles where the water is clean, other than in northern Scotland. They are found through Europe (other than in southern Spain, southern and central Italy, Greece, Norway, northern Sweden and Finland), and through Russia as far as the Ural Mountains.

The Spined Loach

Family COBITIDAE   *Cobitis taenia*

The spined loach (Plate 17) is very similar to the previous species but can be distinguished not only by its smaller size but also by the six barbels of equal length, all of which are rather short. Furthermore it has one erectile spine set in a groove below each eye.

The spined loach is usually 7·5 to 10 cm (3 to 4 in.) and rarely exceeds 13·5 cm (5¼ in.) in length. The colour is lighter than that of the stone loach. The background is yellow and along each side is a line of 10 to 19 roundish spots, sometimes merging into a wide streak. Above this are scattered irregular brownish speckles among which one can usually see another horizontal row of spots. There is a line through the eye and rows of speckles on the dorsal and tail fins.

The spined loach inhabits sandier places than the previous species. It remains concealed in the sand and comes out to feed at night. Also it inhabits slowly flowing and stagnant lowland waters.

The spined loach breeds in April and May. It is rarer than the stone loach and is absent from Scotland, Wales and Ireland, and is found mainly in the Trent, in Cambridgeshire, Wiltshire and Warwickshire. In Europe it is found from Spain, Sicily and Albania northwards to southern Sweden and Finland and also in European Russia.

The Wels

Family SILURIDAE   *Silurus glanis*

This is an eastern European species which has been introduced into Britain and has become naturalised in some waters, such as in the Claydon and Woburn estates.

The wels, or catfish (Plate 24), is olive-green or dark grey-brown above and white below. The sides are mottled with irregular spots. The mouth is large and flattened, with two very long barbels on the snout and four shorter ones on the lower jaw. There is a tiny dorsal fin, very long anal fin and no scales.

The wels grows to an extremely large size in eastern Europe, reaching 5 m (16½ ft) in length and 300 kg (660 lb). The British rod-caught record is 43 lb 8 oz (19·730 kg), although it is said that one over 31 kg (68¼ lb) has been netted in Britain.

In Europe wels live in muddy lakes and large rivers with deep pools. Little is known about their natural history in Britain, but in Europe they breed in April to June in shallow water where the eggs (3 mm in diameter) are deposited in mounds and guarded by the males. The young grow and mature quickly if food is sufficient. Wels are said to be very voracious and eat all kinds of fish, frogs, birds and small mammals. In Britain efforts are being made to prevent them spreading, since the damage they do is almost certainly more than their worth, even in eastern Europe where they are of considerable commercial importance.

Another member of the family SILURIDAE is the American catfish or horned pout *Ictalurus nebulosus*. It is common in North America and

Europe, but has not yet been recorded free in Britain, though it is kept in ponds and aquaria where it only reaches 7 to 10 cm (2¾ to 4 in.). On the Continent it grows to 30 cm (12 in.). It has four long and four shorter barbels and an adipose fin.

The Common Eel

Family ANGUILLIDAE   *Anguilla anguilla*

The shape of the eel (Plate 25) with its long cylindrical body flattened laterally towards the tail, is very well known and is unlikely to be mistaken for any other animal. The pair of fins at once distinguishes it from a snake or lamprey.

Female eels grow to 150 cm (60 in.) and 6 kg (13¼ lb), but no males were observed over 51 cm (20 in.). The British rod-caught record stands at 8 lb 10 oz (3.912 kg) for an eel caught near Bristol in July 1969. The minimum length of mature males is 29 cm (11½ in.) and mature females 42 cm (16½ in.). The colour varies with the state of maturity. The usual colour is dark grey or greenish brown above and yellow below, and these are called 'yellow eels'. However, just before or during migration, they become greyish white to silver with a metallic sheen, and are called 'silver eels'. Eels have no ventral fins, and the dorsal, tail and anal fins are joined. The gill slits are small and the scales are minute.

Eels live in nearly every kind of water, from large lakes and rivers to small ponds and ditches, and they can stand an incredible amount of pollution. The young tend to be in the smaller streams and ditches, often among stones, and the larger eels prefer soft mud. Eels undoubtedly sometimes leave the water and cross land from one piece of water to another.

Eels feed on all kinds of aquatic animals, large and small, dead or alive. They eat insects, snails, worms, crayfish, frogs, fish, small rodents and water birds.

The breeding of eels had for long been a mystery, and it was not until the early 1920's that most of the details had been discovered. It was very well known that migrating silver eels go to sea in late summer or autumn, never to return, and that transparent 'glass eels' 5 to 8 cm (2 to 3¼ in.) long and as thick as a match-stick migrate, when pigmented, as 'elvers' in thousands into fresh water in April or May. It had been established in 1893 that glass eels came from a larval form which had previously been thought to be another animal called *Leptocephalus brevirostris*. A scientist called Schmidt traced the *Leptocephalus* larvae back across the Atlantic, and they become smaller and more numerous as he approached the West Indies. The smallest *Leptocephalus* larvae of 5 to 15 mm were found in the Sargasso Sea at a point half way between

Bermuda and the Leeward Islands. Here the European eels breed, and slightly to the west and south is where the American eels breed. Schmidt found that they take three years to cross to Europe in the North Atlantic Drift, by which time they are still very thin, oval and leaf shaped creatures averaging 7·5 cm (3 in.) in length. These metamorphose (and shrink) to glass eels 6·5 cm (2½ in.) long which turn to elvers and migrate into freshwater. In 1959 Tucker put forward a controversial modification to the accepted story by suggesting that adult European eels die without crossing the Atlantic to spawn, and that all European eels are the progeny of American eels. He explained the slight differences between the two kinds by temperature and current differences in the spawning area. Tucker's brilliantly simple idea neatly overcomes the problem of how the European eel navigates the enormous distances and depths of the ocean to the Sargasso Sea. However, there are many authorities who do not accept Tucker's theory.

The eel is found throughout the entire British Isles. In Europe it is distributed from round the Mediterranean and Black Seas to Scandinavia and Iceland.

The Burbot

Family GADIDAE   *Lota lota*

The burbot (Plate 26) is the only British freshwater representative of the family which includes the important marine species cod, haddock and whiting.

The burbot is covered with large dark brownish spots or marbling, more pronounced on the upper parts, set against a pale yellowish olive background. The belly is a yellowish cream colour. The dark spots are also present on the two dorsal fins, the tail and anal fins. Some specimens are much lighter than others. The body is long and cylindrical with a broad flattened head and laterally flattened tail. There is a short barbel in front of each eye, and a large one on the chin. The pelvic fins are in front of the pectorals. The first dorsal fin is short, and the second dorsal and anal fins are long. The adults range from 30 to 60 cm (12 to 24 in.), or exceptionally 100 cm (40 in.).

Burbot are nocturnal creatures and spend the day in deep water, feeding only at night, so they are not often observed by naturalists. They require reasonably well-oxygenated water and like the bottom of cool clear lakes and rivers.

Burbot breed during the winter from December to March. The eggs, which are about 1·1 mm in diameter, are very numerous, sticky and have an oil globule. They adhere to stones and weeds. The burbot does not feed at spawning time, but at other periods it is very voracious. The young consume larval caddis and other invertebrates, and burbot over 20 cm (8 in.) feed mainly on dead or live small fish, frogs and fish eggs.

In Britain burbot are found in the east coast rivers, but pollution is reducing the places where well-oxygenated, cool, clear water can be found. Although they used to be present from Essex as far north as Durham, they are now very rare. Burbot are not found in Ireland, Scotland or Wales.

Burbot are distributed in Europe from central France and northern Italy in the south as far north as the rivers flowing into the Baltic and Arctic Ocean.

The Bass

Family SERRANIDAE   *Dicentrarchus labrax*

This is strictly a sea fish, but it enters estuaries and rivers in summer.

The bass (Plate 27) has a long streamlined body with two dorsal fins and one anal. The first dorsal has nine spines, the second dorsal one spine, and the anal fin has three. The pelvic fins are immediately below the pectorals. Bass are large fish and can grow to 1 metre (about 40 in.) in length and 12 kg (26½ lb), but British specimens are smaller; the British rod-caught record is 18 lb 2 oz (8·221 kg) for a bass caught off Felixstowe in 1943.

The colour is predominantly a metallic blue above and silvery on the sides and belly. There are sometimes black spots on the young but these are absent from the adults. The opercular and preopercular bones have sharp spines and the fish must be handled with care. The mouth is large and has sharp teeth.

The bass is a coastal fish, but between June and October it enters brackish estuaries and often moves right into fresh water.

Bass breed between May and August, but very little seems to be known about their reproduction with any certainty, and the authorities tend to disagree. Bass are said to spawn in fresh, brackish or salt water. The eggs are 1·15 to 1·20 mm in diameter, and it is said that they float in sea water and sink in fresh water.

Bass eat marine worms, shrimps, prawns and fish. In Britain they are more common off the south coasts and much rarer to the north. The limits of their recorded distribution are from the Black Sea to Stavanger in Norway.

The bass is a great favourite with sea anglers.

The Zander

Family PERCIDAE   *Stizostedion lucioperca*

The zander (Plate 28), or pike-perch as it is often called, is a European fish which has been introduced into restricted localities in England.

The back is greenish grey or bluish olive-green. The sides are olive merging with silvery white on the belly. The back and sides have 8 to 12 darker vertical stripes or blotches, and there are irregular rows of speckles on the dorsal fins. The other fins are pale grey. The body is long, slim and tapered. The head is flattened, with a large mouth and sharp teeth. There are two dorsal fins, the first of which has 13 to 15 spines, and the second has one or two spines and 19 to 23 soft rays.

The zander is usually about 40 to 50 cm (16 to 20 in.) in length. The British rod-caught record stands at 15 lb 5 oz (6·945 kg) for a fish caught in Norfolk in 1968. On the Continent they grow to 130 cm (51 in.) and 12 kg (26½ lb).

The zander inhabits slowly flowing or stagnant water over 2 m (6½ ft) in depth, most often in lakes or rivers. They are sometimes found in brackish water. They breed in April to June near the shore. The eggs are guarded by the males.

Small zander feed on the small drifting crustacea (including *Daphnia*), called zooplankton, and on midges and freshwater shrimps. Large zander eat fish of whatever species is available, and whereas pike swallow fish head first, zander swallow them tail first. The growth is rapid so that in Holland they are 50 cm (20 in.) by four years of age.

The zander has established itself after various introductions, for example in the Claydon Lakes, and in the Great Ouse River system. They originally derive from eastern and central Europe, but are now well established elsewhere, in France, Germany, Denmark and southern Scandinavia.

The Perch

Family PERCIDAE   *Perca fluviatilis*

The perch (Plate 29) is one of our most handsome and best-known coarse fishes and is much sought after by anglers of all ages.

Perch are sedentary fish and do not perform any extensive migrations, though they do seek out deep water in winter, at which time they become very sluggish. In the spring and summer they move into shallow water and can often be seen swimming singly or in shoals near the water's edge or amongst weed.

The upper parts of perch are dark bluish olive-green, grey-green or even mud coloured. The sides are silvery or golden green, and the belly is a silvery white. There are 5 to 9 vertical dark stripes along both sides of the body. Perch have two dorsal fins, the first of which has 13 to 17 sharply pointed spines and a black spot at the rear edge. The second dorsal fin has 1 or 2 spines and 13 to 15 soft branched rays. These two fins are not joined as they are in the ruffe. The dorsal, pectoral and tail fins are greenish grey, but the bottom of the tail, and the whole of the anal and pectoral fins are a bright pinkish red. The eye and mouth are large, and the operculum has one or more sharp spines. The scales are very rough. The body is quite thick and is distinctly hump-backed, particularly in older specimens.

Adult perch grow to between 15 and 30 cm (6

to 12 in.) and the rod-caught record stands at
4 lb 12 oz (2.155 kg), though specimens of 51 cm
(20 in.) and 4·75 kg (10½ lb) have been recorded
from the Continent.

Perch are mainly fish of lakes, ponds, canals
and slow-flowing rivers. They are only rarely
found in swift-running streams.

The breeding season is from late April to June,
when the eggs are laid among plants and twigs
in shallow water. The eggs are joined together
and form an elongated sheet. The larvae hatch
out in seven to ten days depending on the water
temperature. The small fry quickly shoal
amongst weed in the shallow water and feed on
small drifting planktonic crustacea. Medium
sized perch also live in shoals and feed on plankton
and insects as well as bottom living animals such
as insects and freshwater shrimps. The larger
specimens also consume fish of whatever species
is available, and tend to live a more solitary
existence. The male perch are usually smaller
than the females of the same age, and some of
them mature at two years old. The females
on the other hand grow more quickly and first
spawn at three years. Perch can live to an old
age, and specimens of 15 to 20 years are regularly
reported.

The growth of perch is very variable and depends on the water the fish is in. It has been
found in Windermere that the growth through
the summer is connected with the water temperature, which is probably due to the feeding

activity being dependent on the temperature. Some lakes contain very over-crowded populations and it has been shown that a considerable reduction in the numbers can eventually lead to much larger specimens. The growth of many perch seems to fall off above 25 cm (about 10 in.), but those individuals which take to eating fish get a new lease of life and grow to a much larger size.

Perch are well distributed throughout Britain and Ireland, but are absent from the north and west of Scotland. In Europe they are absent from Spain, central and southern Italy, Greece, western Norway and northern Scandinavia. Eastwards they extend to eastern Siberia.

Perch are very good to eat, though only the larger specimens are really worth the effort involved in the preparation. Great care must be taken in handling these fish when they are first caught as the spines are sharp and can cause pain.

The Ruffe

Family PERCIDAE   *Gymnocephalus cernua*

The ruffe or pope (Plate 29) is a small and drab relative of the perch. It can be distinguished from that species by its two dorsal fins, the first one, with 12 to 17 spiny rays, is joined to the second which has 11 to 15 soft branched rays.

The back and flanks of the ruffe are greyish green or muddy olive-brown. The belly is whitish. The back and sides have scattered speckles and irregular blotches. On the dorsal and tail fins the dark spots are in more regular rows. The opercular bones covering the gills have strong sharp spines. The body is less hump-backed than that of the perch.

The length of the ruffe is about 12 to 18 cm (5 to 7 in.). The British rod-caught record stands at 4 oz (113 g) for a fish caught in the River Stour in 1969.

This species is usually found in deep and shady water which is still or slowly flowing. Ruffe congregate in shoals near the shore at night, but tend to hide during the day.

Ruffe breed from March to May, and it has been said that the eggs are extruded intermittently. The eggs, which have an oil globule, and are 1 mm in diameter, are laid among weed along the shore and hatch after about 9 to 14 days. This fish is very fecund; a ruffe of 18·7 cm (7¼ in. approx.) has been reported to contain 104,000 eggs.

After the young have grown through a plankton eating stage, the ruffe live on all kinds of small aquatic animals such as insect larvae and freshwater shrimps, as well as worms.

Ruffe are not widely distributed in Britain. They are absent from Scotland, Wales and Ireland, and in England they are found mainly in the Midlands as far north as mid Yorkshire and

Lancashire. They are found through northern
and central Europe, from north-eastern France
to the Baltic, where they enter brackish water,
and in the rivers flowing into the White Sea.
They extend eastwards to Siberia.

The Large-mouthed Black Bass

Family CENTRARCHIDAE   *Micropterus salmoides*

This species, which has been introduced from
North America, has become naturalised in a few
localities (Surrey and Dorset), but they do not
prosper.

The upper parts are grey-green or slate
coloured, and the sides are olive-green with dark
mottling. The first dorsal fin, which has 9 or
10 spiny rays, is lower than the second which
has one spine and 12 or 13 soft branched
rays. The fins are almost separated by a
deep notch (Plate 28). The young have a
longitudinal stripe or row of spots along the
body. This species grows to 40 to 60 cm (16
to 24 in.).

The breeding time is from March to July,
when the female prepares an area 1 m (3 ft
approx.) in diameter, and this is covered with
vegetation. After the eggs have been laid and
fertilised on this nest, they are aerated and
guarded by the male until after they have
hatched. The food of the adults consists of

bottom invertebrates as well as small fish, frogs and tadpoles.

In the small-mouthed black bass *Micropterus dolomieu*, which has also been introduced from America, the dorsal fins are more completely joined, and the upper jaw does not reach the hind edge of the eye, whereas in the large-mouthed species the upper jaw does reach the eye margin, and even exceeds it in adults.

The Grey Mullets

Family MUGILIDAE

There are three British species of grey mullets and they resemble each other very closely indeed. Furthermore, very little is known about the differences in their life histories, so in this account we will first see how they are differentiated, and then treat them as one aggregate species.

The species are:

The thick-lipped grey mullet	*Crenimugil labrosus*
The thin-lipped grey mullet	*Chelon ramada*
The golden grey mullet	*Chelon auratus*

If specimens of all three species are together so that they can be contrasted and compared side by side, it is easy to separate them, but if only one is present its identification often baffles even the expert.

In the thin- and thick-lipped species (Plate 30) the back is a steel blue or metallic blue-green and the flanks are a similar colour but paler, whereas in the golden grey mullet the back is browner, the sides are buff, and the whole fish has a golden rather than a steely sheen with golden spots on the sides of the head. In the thin-lipped species the thickness of the lips is less than half the width of the eye, whereas in the thick-lipped species the thickness is more than half the eye width. There are also differences in the relative positions of the dorsal and anal fins, but the general naturalist should preserve specimens of these fish and send them to an expert for identification.

The belly of all species is buff. The first dorsal fin has four spines and the second, which is some way behind, has one spine and eight or nine soft rays.

These species are essentially sea fish which enter estuaries in shoals during summer and autumn, and go up rivers. They are most often seen in docks and round piers and jetties. In the late autumn they return to the sea. They are extremely adept at escaping capture and if they cannot find a way under or round a seine net, they will leap over the head rope, and where one has gone the rest of the shoal will follow.

Mullet feed on bottom mud and soil with small particles of plants and animals. Up to 85% of the stomach contents may be indigestible, and the extraction of nutriment requires very long intestines, and it is said that a 33 cm (13 in.) grey mullet has intestines 213 cm (7 ft) long.

Grey mullet can grow to a large size and specimens of 40 to 50 cm (16 to 20 in.) are not uncommon and some up to 90 cm (about 3 ft) have been recorded. The British rod-caught record stands at 10 lb 1 oz (4·564 kg) for a specimen caught off Portland in 1952.

Very little is known at present about the breeding of grey mullet in Britain, but spawning is said to take place in April and May, and so far only one spawning place, off the Scilly Isles, is known.

The grey mullets are mainly southern species and for the most part enter estuaries on the southern and western coasts. In Europe they are found from the Black Sea to southern Sweden, Trondheim in Norway and southern Iceland. The thick-lipped species is the most northern ranging, and the golden grey mullet the most southern species (rarely reaching Denmark or Scotland). They are found down the Atlantic African coast as far as the Cape of Good Hope.

The Bullhead

Family COTTIDAE   *Cottus gobio*

The bullhead, or miller's thumb (Plate 31) as it is sometimes called, is a small freshwater member of a family that has many marine representatives, some of which grow to a considerable size.

The bullhead very rarely exceeds 10 cm (4 in.), and large specimens are usually around 6 to 8 cm ($2\frac{1}{4}$ to $3\frac{1}{8}$ in.). It is a flattened, bottom living fish with a large broad head and mouth and a tapering body. The pectoral fins are large and the tail fin is rounded. There is one anal and two dorsal fins, the second of which is much longer than the first. The rays of the first dorsal fin are spiny but the others are soft.

Bullheads are usually dark grey or brown with darker speckles and marbling. The flanks are paler and the belly is a creamy yellow. The dorsal, tail and pectoral fins have spots arranged in bands. The gill covers are spiny and the fish has to be handled with great care. The body is covered with a tough skin, and there are no scales.

The bullhead spends most of its time sheltering beneath stones, and most naturalists pottering about along the edge of a rocky river or lake have probably disturbed these fish which flee from one hole to another like mice. They are not able to swim very far. In these shallow water areas the bullheads spawn between February and May. The eggs are deposited in a mass on the undersides of stones where they are then guarded by the male for about a month until they hatch. Bullheads prefer clear well-oxygenated water and feed on small crustacea such as freshwater shrimps and aquatic insects. They are well distributed through England and Wales, but are very rare in Scotland and absent from Ireland. In Europe they are present from southern France to the Arctic sea coast, and eastwards to the Ural Mountains.

The Three-spined Stickleback

Family GASTEROSTEIDAE   *Gasterosteus aculeatus*

The sticklebacks must be some of our best-known freshwater fishes and are certainly often caught by children when fishing for tiddlers. Sticklebacks make very good aquarium fish, but they tend to be extremely pugnacious, particularly at the spawning season in early summer.

The three-spined stickleback (Plate 31) is a small fish usually of 4 to 6 cm ($1\frac{1}{2}$ to $2\frac{1}{2}$ in.) and only exceptionally over 10 cm (4 in.) in length.

This species is unlikely to be confused with any other fish. It has three dorsal spines in front of the dorsal fin and the pelvic fins are spiny. The skin has no scales but there are vertical bony plates on the sides of the body. The eye is large. The spindle-shaped body tapers to a long narrow part in front of the rounded tail fin.

The upper parts are blue-black or greenish, and paler below. At the spawning time the male takes on a brilliant red belly and flanks, and a bright green back. The female becomes yellower.

Three-spined sticklebacks live in stagnant or flowing water, often in enormous shoals. They are found mainly in fresh water but also they are common in salt water, particularly in brackish dykes and rock pools. In some places they are found in the open sea. They have been reported from some very extraordinary places, such as from an artesian well 128 metres deep.

At the spawning time, which is in May and June, they migrate upstream, or into fresher water. The male takes up, and pugnaciously defends, a territory. In this territory he makes a nest out of bits of vegetation and detritus, bound together with sticky threads that are secreted by the kidneys. At this time the kidneys become enlarged to carry out this rather odd additional function. When the nest has been built, the male entices females into it to lay their eggs, and a number of females may lay in the same nest. After the eggs are laid the male guards the eggs and fans a current of water over them until the young hatch and are able to fend for themselves. Sometimes the male makes additional holes in the nest to increase the current over the eggs and so keep them well aerated.

This species eats small worms, insects and crustacea such as *Daphnia*. They in turn are eaten by a very large number of other fish.

The three-spined stickleback is found throughout the British Isles but rarely in Ireland and north Scotland. It is found over most of western Europe north of the Mediterranean, to Scandinavia, Iceland and Greenland, as well as over much of North America.

The Ten-spined Stickleback

Family GASTEROSTEIDAE   *Pungitius pungitius*

This species is very similar to the three-spined stickleback, but is slimmer and has 10 dorsal spines (occasionally 8, 9 or 11) in front of the dorsal fin (Plate 31). It is also a smaller species reaching 3 to 6 cm (1¼ to 2½ in.) and exceptionally 9 cm (3½ in.).

The colour of the back is blue-green or greenish yellow, and the belly is silvery white. Occasionally spots or speckles are discernible. During the breeding season the throat and belly of the male turn black. The dorsal fin is situated in line above the anal. The pelvic fin consists of a single spine and one soft ray. The body tapers markedly to the tail.

The habitat of the ten-spined stickleback is more confined to fresh water than that of the previous species, but the food of the two is very similar. The breeding behaviour only differs in some details. Whereas the nest of the three-spined stickleback is situated on the bottom in a depression in the sand, the males of the present species prefer to build their nests hanging from water plants. The eggs are only 1 mm in diameter compared with 1·6 mm in the three-spined species.

The ten-spined stickleback is found in Kent, Surrey, East Anglia, the east midlands, Anglesey, round Lough Neagh and the Clyde area and sporadically elsewhere. It is said to be rare in Ireland. It is a more lowland species than the three-spined stickleback.

The Flounder

Family PLEURONECTIDAE   *Platichthys flesus*

Even experienced naturalists and professional freshwater biologists are often amazed how far into fresh water the flounder can penetrate. The flounder (Plate 32) is a flatfish related to the marine plaice and dab. These fish are not flattened so that they lie on their stomach, but they are thin fish which lie on their sides. In the case of the flounder they mostly lie on the left side, though an occasional specimen is found lying on the right side. When it first hatches from the egg, the flounder is symmetrical like other fish but after some time the left eye moves over the head to the right side, and the fish lies down on its left side. This underside is white and only the upper right side is pigmented.

The body is oval and olive-green or brown with orange spots on the body and fins. The upper surface has rough scales or small spines by the gill cover, and down the lateral line, and along the bases of the fringing fins. This feature immediately distinguishes the flounder from any other marine flatfish. It is very unlikely that the flounder could be confused with any freshwater fish. Occasionally a specimen is found which has patches of sandy pigmentation on the white side.

Flounders are usually 30 to 35 cm (12 to 14 in.), but sometimes they reach 45 cm (18 in.).

The British rod-caught record is for one caught at Fowey in 1956 at 5 lb 11½ oz (2·594 kg).

Flounders are very fecund, and they breed in the sea in spring from January to April. The almost transparent eggs float in the surface waters. The eggs hatch in a week or ten days depending on the temperature, and the larvae drift in the plankton for some time before seeking the bottom. The young flounders move inshore and migrate into fresh water. They move up the rivers and into lakes and lochs, but they cannot successfully negotiate waterfalls. They remain in fresh water until mature, at about three years of age. These adults return to the sea to spawn and thereafter do not penetrate quite so far into freshwater as the immature youngsters.

The food in the sea consists of marine worms and cockles, and in fresh water it is made up of insect larvae, snails and crustacea, worms and small fish.

Flounders are found all round the British coasts and inland from there to the first obstruction or pollution. In Europe they are found from the Black Sea and Mediterranean to the Baltic, Scandinavia and the Arctic Ocean.

Although large numbers are eaten, they are not really so appetising as their relative the plaice, or some of the other flatfish.

Index

137